GEMS No. 1:
The primary purpose rule in British immigration law

Sanjiv Sachdeva

with a Foreword by Ian Macdonald QC

TRENTHAM BOOKS
GEMS
★★★

Trentham Books and School of Oriental & African Studies

First published in 1993 by Trentham Books Limited

Trentham Books Limited
Westview House
734 London Road
Oakhill
Stoke-on-Trent
Staffordshire
England ST4 5NP

British Library Cataloguing Publication Data
A catalogue record for this book is available from the British Library.

ISBN: 0 948080 98 1

Designed and typeset by Trentham Print Design Limited and printed in Great Britain by BPCC Wheatons Ltd, Exeter.

Ethnic Minority Studies at SOAS

is a new series of small monographs and collected papers that focus on current issues in the study of ethnic minorities in Britain and elsewhere in the world.

The series is edited by Dr Werner F. Menski, Senior Lecturer in South Asian Laws at the School of Oriental and African Studies and the Chairman of GEMS, the Group for Ethnic Minority Studies at the School.

No.1 Sanjiv Sachdeva
The primary purpose rule in British immigration law.

Table of Contents

Foreword by Ian Macdonald, QC   vii

Preface by Werner F. Menski   1
The primary purpose rule: Dimensions of the problem

Chapter 1: The primary purpose rule in its wider context   7

Chapter 2: British immigration law in the 20th century   13
  2.1 **British immigration law up to 1971**   14
    2.1.1 Developments up to 1945   14
    2.1.2 Post-War immigration to Britain   17
    2.1.3 The Commonwealth Immigrants Act, 1962   20
    2.1.4 The Commonwealth Immigrants Act, 1968   23
  2.2 **An unwelcome addition: The Ugandan Asians**   26
  2.3 **British immigration law under the 1971 Act**   27
  2.4 **The status of the Immigration Rules at law**   29
  2.5 **The development of immigration law after the 1971 Act** 31
  2.6 **The Immigration Act, 1988**   39

Chapter 3: Origins and development of the primary purpose rule   43
  3.1 **The position prior to the Immigration Act, 1971**   44
  3.2 **The role of the Immigration Act, 1971**   51
  3.3 **The rules between 1974 and 1977: Balancing immigration** 52
    consequences and hardship
  3.4 **Marriages of convenience and immigration law**   55
  3.5 **The formal introduction of the primary purpose rule** 61
    3.5.1 The perceived need for tighter immigration control 62
    3.5.2 The Immigration Rules of 1980 (HC 394)   66
    3.5.3 The application of the primary purpose rule 69
    3.5.3.1 The undercover development of the primary purpose rule 70
    3.5.3.2 The requirement to have met: Attacking arranged 74
      marriages
    3.5.3.3 The pressure from Europe   80
    3.5.3.4 The Immigration Rules of 1986 (HC169)   84
    3.5.3.5 The full-fledged application of the primary purpose rule 89
      after 1983
    3.5.3.6 The rule changes of 1985 (HC503)   91
    3.5.3.7 Recent developments: Finetuning exclusionary 100
      mechanisms

Chapter 4: The case-law on the primary purpose rule   107

  4.1 The ambivalent early approach to South Asian marriages   108

  4.2 Marriages of convenience and primary purpose   112

  4.3 The early case-law and its effects   119

  4.4 Tightening the screws: Vinod Bhatia   122

  4.5 The post-Bhatia conundrum   128

  4.6 Intervening devotion: a fresh attempt to make sense of   130
      'primary purpose'

  4.7 Post-Arun Kumar realism   134

  4.8 Seeking to establish guidelines: Hoque and Singh   139

  4.9 The waning of judicial sympathy   149

  4.10 The dangers of pleading love   159

  4.11 Relief from Europe?   165

Appendix: Chronological list of Immigration Rules 1973-1990   171

Index of Cases   173

Table of Statutes   177

Bibliography   179

Foreword

Ian Macdonald QC

It is always a pleasure to welcome a new study, a new author, or a new series of publications. Here all three are combined in this single volume.

The new author is to be congratulated on his first sortie into print. His writing has maturity, depth and understanding allied with commendable scholarship but the author does not discard entirely the raw edge of his indignation at what he has found in the trough of despond created by the primary purpose rule.

I have written and spoken much about the primary purpose rule. So have others. There are many pamphlets, speeches, determinations and judgements but this is the first book devoted to an in depth examination of the rule. The book deals with its history as well as the details of its content and sets it well into the context of immigration law and practice as well.

An in depth examination of the rule does not improve it. If anything it confirms its major characteristic — that it is selectively aimed, that it divides families unnecessarily and cruelly, and that it is unworkable. In the very legitimate outcry against its existence, the very real problem of the reluctant bride or fiancée is ignored.

Immigration law now qualifies as a branch of law on its own. It has its own appeal tribunals, law reports and text books. It features more often in Judicial Review than any other branch of law. It is a major plank of EEC law. It is no longer right to treat it as a subdivision of constitutional or administrative law. As it grows and develops it is increasingly going to produce subtexts on particular aspects of it: refugees, EEC free movement rights and so forth. The production of this volume by Sanjiv Sachdeva can be seen as one such development. Hopefully it will be used widely in colleges and universities as a teaching tool, but it will also be of use to administrators, adjudicators and practitioners.

Preface

The primary purpose rule: Dimensions of the problem

Werner F. Menski

The primary purpose rule is quite obviously a central element of current British immigration control. It may be an unworkable rule in practice, but it has quite apparently been purposely designed and is constantly refined to prevent the development of a rational system of ascertaining the claims of individuals for entry to the UK. This was done, *inter alia*, by leaving maximum scope for the discretion of those who consider the cases of potential immigrants, creating insurmountable obstacles for applicants and their advisers.

There can be no doubt that the primary purpose rule seeks to exclude a particular category of people who have been contributing most conspicuously to the numbers of recent immigrants to the UK. The rule's primary purpose appears to be to prevent the use of marriage as a means of obtaining settlement rights in Britain. While this rule could apply to any spouses, it has been selectively aimed at people coming to Britain from certain parts of the world. Thus, the primary purpose rule has affected mainly spouses seeking entry from the Indian subcontinent, but more recent evidence shows very clearly that the harsh effects of the rule are also felt by other non-white ethnic minority groups, in particular people from Nigeria, Ghana and some Caribbean countries.

The actual operation of this rule impinges directly on widely shared perceptions of civil liberties and human dignity and the literature is full of angry comments about the racist and cruel nature of this rule. The present legal position certainly casts doubts upon the extent of compliance by the UK with European and other international instruments and guarantees on human rights.

This situation has caused considerable anguish, not only in the directly affected communities and families, but also among leading members of the legal profession who have become involved in immigration law as a dimension

1

of human rights law in general (see for example Macdonald and Blake 1991:vii). The individual's helplessness in view of insurmountable legal hurdles has been expressed probably most clearly by those members of ethnic minority communities who have been called upon to administer this inhuman rule. Thus, Anver Jeevanjee, a member of an Immigration Appeal Tribunal, in the unreported case of *Mohammad Shahban* v. *Visa Officer, Islamabad* (6996) stated:

> 'I am afraid that it has yet again become necessary for me as a lay member of the Immigration Appeal Tribunal and indeed as a member of what is referred to as 'ethnic minority' in Britain to disagree with the factual issues of primary purpose of marriage as applied by my majority colleagues... I feel that to fail to oppose the dismissal of this appeal would be tantamount to endorse the denial of justice to the appellants and a lack of compassion, whatever the legal arguments.

> The law imposed by Parliament apparently establishes equality for all. However, it seems to me that in its application, cultural differences, interpretation, prejudices, generalisations etc. leave much to be desired.

> ...It would seem to me unjust to pick and choose from the evidence what one prefers to fit into a preconceived notion. This places the appellant's side in an insurmountable situation irrespective of the truthfulness of their evidence. Likewise there is a 'no win' situation whether appellants' replies to the entry clearance officer on the crucial issue of primary purpose are damaging or not.'

Unfortunately, the 'no win' situation that Mr. Jeevanjee describes has been the pattern of so many cases that even experienced legal practitioners have become frustrated in their efforts to guide clients through the minefields of tricky questions and self-incriminating answers. Textbook writers have emphasised the need to avoid a situation where an application has been refused (see Mole 1987:4). For, once a case gets entangled in the appeals system, not only does this mean long delays, but it becomes also virtually impossible to convince those deciding cases that it was not the applicant's primary purpose to come to Britain when s/he married or got engaged to a person settled here.

The legal core element of the primary purpose rule is that the application of a male or female spouse or fiancé(e) for settlement in this country should be refused if the primary purpose of the marriage is to obtain entry into the UK. A crucial contributory factor to the 'no win' situation in primary purpose cases is the fact that the onus of proof rests upon the applicant to satisfy the Entry Clearance Officer (if abroad) or the Secretary of State (if applying to stay from within the UK) that it was not the primary purpose of the marriage to gain entry.

In recent years, accompanied by much stricter maintenance and accommodation requirements in particular (see now Gillespie 1992), the primary purpose rule has been an effective means of reducing the number of persons coming to Britain from certain parts of the world (for statistics see for example Banton 1988:90). It appears that successive governments have viewed the standing the attitudes and policy issues of that time. The fact that such a report was produced at all indicates that the topic had assumed particular significance for politicians as well as policy makers.

The Report itself was preoccupied with the perceived need to 'batten down the hatches' more securely against Commonwealth immigration. Commentators have detected an almost obsessive concern to find further ways of tightening immigration controls (see Bevan 1986:84). It is significant that among the major recommendations of the Report were a Government declaration against any more primary immigration, an annual quota for entrants from the Indian subcontinent, priority in admission for wives and children, and suggestions that in future children should only be admitted before they reach the age of 12. Further recommendations, not surprisingly, related to the need for more resources to catch up with overstayers and illegal entrants, and to the tightening of identity checks by social service departments, as well as a more general inquiry into a system of internal controls.

The Government's response to the Report (contained in Cmnd. 7287 of 1978) was initially unenthusiastic. It rejected the proposals for a system of internal control, an annual quota for entrants from the Indian subcontinent and the entry of children only under the age of 12, which was regarded as inhumane. On the other hand, most of the Report's suggestions have in fact subsequently been implemented by changes in the Immigration Rules in 1980 (H.C. 394) and 1983 (H.C. 169) and by administrative means, such as the introduction of priority queues and DSS identity checks. It is also surely no coincidence that the tightening of the entire system of immigration control relating to husbands and fiancés was gradually achieved during the 1980s.

It has been argued that the 1978 Report understated and undervalued the importance of race relations due to its fixation on the issue of immigration (Bevan 1986:85). The public debate on immigration at this time aired the well-worn themes of apprehension about immigration, but also showed the close link with race relations issues. Bevan (1986:85) reports how a controversial acquittal under the incitement to racial hatred provisions in section 6 of the *Race Relations Act*, 1965 caused tempers to rise. In view of the weak position of the race relations law at that time (see in detail Lester and Bindman 1972:343-374), the bad feelings generated arose perhaps not so much out of the fact of acquittal of the racist offender as from the observations of the presiding judge, who in summing-up wished the accused well and seemed to condone what he had done:

'Of course, we cannot accommodate here unlimited numbers of immigrants coming into this country, but it is not something to be ashamed of... houses are scarce. It is said that immigrants will occupy homes which are needed by ordinary English folk in this country. Members of the jury, those are matters upon which people are entitled to hold and declare strong views expressed in moderate terms.' (quoted in Bevan 1986:85).

The well-used drawbridge approach to immigration, which underlies these sentiments, was re-iterated by the then Leader of the Opposition:

'People are really rather afraid that this country might be rather swamped by people with a different culture and you know, the British character has done so much for democracy, for law, and done so much throughout the world that if there is any fear that it might be swamped people are going to react and be rather hostile to them coming in. So, if you want good race relations, you have got to allay people's fear on numbers.' (Mrs. Margaret Thatcher M.P. in *H.C. Debates*, [31 January 1978], col.240).

The above statement contains familiar themes of immigration control, such as the emotive concept of 'being swamped', the need to preserve the British character — whatever that may be — from dilution and corruption, and again a reference to the link of immigration control with good race relations.

While there appears to have been some recognition of the fact that no British government could possibly claim to wish to end immigration altogether (Bevan 1986:86), the measures highlighted and advocated in the 1978 All-Party Select Committee Report were more or less completely incorporated within the Conservative Election Manifesto of 1979. The suggested changes included a recommendation that the admission of husbands, fiancés and more distant relatives should be permitted only in exceptional circumstances. The years 1980 (H.C. 394) and 1983 (H.C. 169) saw changes in the Immigration Rules, concentrating on a 'fine-tuning' of existing controls, including new rules on the admission of spouses, to whom we shall turn in detail in chapter 3.

In terms of an actual reduction in the number of entrants, the effects of these rule changes have, at least initially, been seen as marginal. Bevan (1986:86-87) explains that a continuing commitment to family reunion, which is probably inescapable on human rights grounds, cannot be made to be compatible with the aim to reduce numbers. Moreover, the argument that immigration control is essential as a defence mechanism for the preservation of the 'British character' overlooks, as indicated already, the demographic realities of Britain during the 1970s, with a substantial 'coloured' population that is continuously increased not only by immigration, but also by natural growth. In this situation, as Bevan (1986:86-87) has rightly emphasised, politicians can only hope to make the right noises: it is neither politically feasible to call for an end to immigration nor to advocate less stringent immigration controls. As many times before, politicians of all persuasions appear to be driven by public opinion rather than acting as moral leaders in this difficult area of public interest, though it could equally be argued that many politicians would appear to share the xenophobic views of certain sections of the electorate.

A major reform during the 1980s has been a complete overhaul of the British nationality law, which does not concern us here in detail, but is quite relevant to developments in British immigration law in the 1980s and thereafter. On 1 January 1983, the *British Nationality Act*, 1981 came into force. This Act effectively recast British citizenship and abandoned the existing definition of patriality, so that corresponding amendments to the *Immigration Act*, 1971 became inevitable.

The 1981 Act (the leading authority on this is Fransman 1989) focuses on the concept of 'right of abode' and defines this right in terms of the new categories of British citizenship created by the Act. In essence, a re-classification of the CUKCs under the 1948 Act was introduced, leading to three major categories of British citizens, namely British citizens, British Dependent Territories citizens, and British Overseas citizens (see Fransman 1989:141). The right of abode and full British citizenship are to be more or less equated, while the other categories of British citizenship do not confer the right of abode in the UK.

An important feature of this Act is that it abolished citizenship by birth in the UK. Children born in the UK after commencement of the Act will only become British citizens if one of their parents is a British citizen or is settled in the UK. The government's reasons for abolishing the pure *jus soli* principle were (i) that it feared abuse by those who came to the UK for the express purpose of having their child acquire British citizenship, and (ii) that it was undesirable that children born in the UK to parents who were only there for temporary periods and purposes should obtain an indefinite right of re-entry without having any substantial connection with the UK. Fear of future immigration is, therefore, a major if not the main motivating factor behind what are quite substantial recent changes in British nationality law.

The early 1980s were a period of little change in British immigration law with respect to the development of further statutory provisions. As we shall see below in chapter 3, the focus of attention has shifted to the judicial arena.

In 1985 the Commission for Racial Equality [CRE] published its only major investigation so far in the field of immigration, a detailed report, entitled *Immigration Control Procedures* (Commission for Racial Equality 1985). This formal investigation by the CRE was initiated because of the discovery that virginity tests had been carried out in 1979 on Indian fiancées at Heathrow Airport (see Lal and Wilson 1986:49-51). The CRE decided that an investigation would assist in the elimination of racial discrimination, though this prompted the Home Office to try to veto the investigation (see *Home Office* v. *Commission for Racial Equality* [1982] Q.B. 385).

Probably as a result of the disputes over it in the first place, the Report is most difficult to obtain; not even the CRE library appears to hold a copy of it. The Report itself does not really disclose many factual details, though it focuses on the operation of the immigration control procedures. However, the Report concluded that British immigration controls were being operated too strictly under the excuse of having to 'weed out' ineligible entrants (for some details see also Bevan 1986:88-89). The CRE clearly felt that this was to the detriment of race relations, and also unfair to genuinely eligible entrants (for a good example of this see Lal and Wilson 1986:8-22, esp. 13-14; also Sondhi 1987). The Report brought to light evidence that immigration authorities had an 'uncompromisingly suspicious attitude' (Bevan 1986:88) towards passengers from certain countries, which often gave rise to considerable hardship:

'The heavy emphasis on excluding the ineligible rather than giving prompt and sympathetic attention to the rights of the eligible has led to administrative practices which, in the Commission's view, bear with particularly adverse effect on people from the New Commonwealth, Pakistan and other Third World countries. The official explanation for this is the 'pressure to emigrate' argument.' (Commission for Racial Equality 1985:v).

Perhaps the most significant feature of this Report, apart from the fact that it is the most independent and searching survey of British immigration control so far conducted, is its investigation into areas which have by long tradition remained secret and sensitive to civil servants. The CRE gained access to internal administrative instructions which guide immigration officers in their duties, and the Report quoted from them extensively. This led the Home Secretary to announce in *The Times* and *The Guardian* of 13 April 1985 that these instructions were under review and that future versions might be published. The Government's initial reaction to the Report can also be studied at *H.C. Debates* ([23 May 1985], col.1168). As the conclusions to the Report, in particular, emphasise very clearly (at pp. 125ff.), the CRE were keen to push for a fairer and more equitable treatment of applicants, on the basis that this could bring substantial benefits to race relations (see also Bevan 1986:88). It has been argued, though, that this is a doubtful result:

'The level of racial discrimination has been so entrenched that a relaxation of immigration procedures would come so late as to improve race relations marginally, if at all. From the viewpoint of the resident immigrant population it would probably be seen as a cosmetic operation, implemented, significantly, now that large scale immigration has passed. To have effect such a change in emphasis would have to be accompanied by a concerted and wide ranging attack on racial discrimination, an attack which no Government or Opposition has been prepared to mount.' (Bevan 1986:88-89).

As indicated above, the CRE Report showed that the Home Office worked on the principle that evasion of immigration controls is most prevalent amongst entrants from countries where there is the greatest economic, political or social pressure to leave (on such factors see in detail Rose et al. 1969:43ff.). The fact that a large number of apprehended evaders come from poor countries is, the Report argues, due to biased methods of detection and the stereotyping of those nationalities as likely evaders. Bevan (1986:89) has criticised this conclusion as 'highly debatable'.

The CRE Report itself did concede that the above factors may be underlying reasons for emigration. As the greater number of primary immigrants in the 1950s and 1960s came from particular countries, it is only logical that the greatest pressure of secondary immigrants will arise in those countries; when faced with the inflexible nature of the UK's immigration laws, the temptation to evade control will be sizeable. But the CRE Report emphasised the negative effects on race relations in Britain of a stereotyping of all persons from certain countries as fraudulent evaders of controls:

'We did not find that this argument was justified by reliable statistical or other evidence. Yet it continues to inform official thinking and action.' (CRE 1985:v).

It could, however, be argued that if the Home Office can detect so many evaders by stereotyping, the temptation may be to increase rather than decrease the extent of the stereotyping (Bevan 1986:89). The CRE Report, however, emphasised the rather negative impact on the ethnic minorities resident in Britain:

'The effects of the operation of immigration control on ethnic minorities raises fundamental questions, for them and for others, about their place in British society, and the fairness or otherwise of the treatment they can expect here. This in turn affects the state of race relations.' (CRE 1985:v).

Bevan, the only author who makes extensive use of the CRE Report, clearly shares the general attitude of the Report's conclusions, which call for a more open-minded approach to the situation of individual immigrants, for natural justice and, more generally, for a less hostile attitude to immigration and a positive commitment by the Government to improving race relations. The Report emphasises in particular the need for families of non-white UK citizens to be able to live together without undue delay or hindrance.

Prior to the CRE Report, the Home Office had published a study entitled *The Work of the Immigration and Nationality Department* (1984). Bevan, perhaps in an attempt to put the Government's side, reminds us of statistics given for the year 1983, when 35 million passengers arrived at UK ports, 12 million were subject to control, yet only 14,665 were refused leave to enter. This means that only 0.12% of all people subject to control were actually refused leave to enter (Bevan 1986:89). On the basis of these figures, Bevan argues that a relaxation in the UK's immigration procedures would hardly open a 'floodgate', a conclusion that was also reached by the CRE Report.

If we return briefly to the changes in the law itself, we see that the development of immigration law throughout the 1980s has followed the pattern of successive tightening of perceived or actual loopholes. Thus, on 1 September 1986, the Home Secretary announced that citizens of Bangladesh, Ghana, India, Nigeria and Pakistan would in future be required to obtain a visa in order to gain admission to the UK as visitors. This step meant that entry clearance had in future to be obtained from outside the UK, i.e., normally in the country of origin. This measure was considered very successful:

'Although the Foreign and Commonwealth Office was apparently opposed to the introduction of visa initially, both it and the Home Office now appear to be well pleased with the arrangements which the Government had introduced to tackle the 'chaos' at major UK ports of entry, notably Terminal 3, Heathrow. In the 1987 Home Office Report on the work of the Immigration, Nationality and Passports Departments, the Minister of State, Timothy Renton, reported: 'I have been impressed by the manner in which these new arrangements have been put into successful operation. Queues at British Airports have diminished and, as I saw for myself on a recent trip to the Indian subcontinent, the vast majority of applications are dealt with on the day the application is received. Regular travellers from these countries, equipped with multiple entry visas appreciate the speed with which they now pass through the control in Britain'.' (quoted in Drabu and Bowen 1989:7).

The very short notice with which the visa system was introduced precluded the possibility of it being subjected to any critical examination. Nor did the Government provide any detailed information as to how the system is actually working. However, according to a number of reports in the British ethnic minority press, applicants from all five countries concerned have been facing considerable delays in receiving visas. There have also been many complaints that visa holders from these countries have been refused admission at UK ports of entry and were again subjected to searching enquiries.

Researchers from the United Kingdom Immigrants Advisory Service (UKIAS) who visited visa officers in the five countries concerned, after examining both the records and experiences of visa applicants and visa holders who had been refused admission at UK ports of entry, found that the so-called 'same day' system of granting visas was maintained simply by turning away applicants at the end of each day. Consequently this high number of deferrals results in applicants having to turn up on another day, thereby facing substantial delays, increased costs and inconvenience. The ministerial claims that 90 per cent of all applications are dealt with the same day do not, therefore, stand up to close examination (Drabu and Bowen 1989:5). The researchers found that at the UK ports of entry immigration officers were exercising their powers of detention if there was the slightest chance or suspicion that the visa may have been obtained by misrepresentation or concealment of material facts. The information gathered points to the visa system as having become a two-class system. Not surprisingly it is the wealthy and the privileged who have less difficulties in obtaining visas and gaining entry, whereas the less well-off are subject to delays while Entry Clearance Officers undertake unnecessary paperwork in checking the records of applicants and their sponsors (Drabu and Bowen 1989:5).

The above Report sees the visa system as representing an additional tightening of the immigration control system, on the pretext that visitors from the five countries concerned are under greater pressure to emigrate and to evade controls than visitors from wealthier parts of the world, which is a theme following on from the 1985 CRE Report (see CRE 1985:72ff.).

Michael Day, the current Chairman of the CRE, has commented on the visa rules as follows:

'It is in the interest of good race relations to ensure that the visa system does not set aside nor hinder the rights of genuine visitors. The... report therefore makes a strong case for a shift in administrative priorities towards greater emphasis on the rights of those applicants who are eligible for visas, and for the law to be equitably administered.' (Drabu and Bowen 1989:5).

However, when one considers that the possession of a visa or entry certificate carries with it a presumption of eligibility for admission, but does not guarantee that the holder will be granted leave to enter, the scope for discretion of the immigration officers at the port of entry is perhaps too large. On arrival in Britain, a further examination by an officer may last several hours, or even days. It is powers such as these, and of course abuse of these powers, which cast a bad light on the UK's immigration control procedures. One is also forced to wonder about the efficiency of these procedures when:

> 'Although most visa applicants are interviewed within no more than a week by the Entry Clearance Officers abroad, it often takes up to a year before an appeal is heard and determined in the U.K., thus effectively defeating the purpose of the visit, particularly in cases where the appellant wished to attend a wedding, funeral or to see a sick relative.' (UKIAS 1988:6).

The 1986-87 Annual Report of the same organisation gives examples of applicants who had what appeared to be good professional reasons for being granted a visa, but were subsequently refused: for example, a sports reporter from a regional newspaper in Bangladesh who wished to cover the England vs Pakistan test series; a chess grandmaster who planned to play in an international tournament and an Imam due to officiate temporarily at a mosque in Birmingham which was without its own Imam during one of the holy months of the year (for details see UKIAS 1987:7). If even temporary visits are viewed with such suspicion and receive such negative responses, how much less hope of a sympathetic approach is there for persons who wish to actually settle in the UK and state this in an open and straightforward manner? The developments of British immigration law during the 1980s have not given much reassurance to those members of ethnic minorities resident in Britain who wish to enjoy family life in the country of their choice. In other words, the warnings and recommendations of the 1985 CRE Report have not been taken seriously.

■ 2.6 The Immigration Act, 1988

This Act continues the official approach of seeking to curb certain perceived abuses of the immigration law, but it goes even further in terms of cultural interference. The 1988 Act is the most recent amendment of the *Immigration Act*, 1971. It is a very short Act, which was clearly designed to tackle very specific points. Timothy Renton M.P., the Minister at the Home Office responsible for the Bill, described the proposals as making 'sensible and limited changes to ensure that our immigration law remains flexible and effective' and that 'the present Bill does no more than reinforce the framework of the 1971 Act in a number of limited respects which the passage of time has made necessary' (Blake and Scannell 1988:2). Such comments have been criticised as cruelly misleading (Blake and Scannell 1988:2).

Some of the main provisions of the Act, which came into force on 10 July 1988, are as follows: Section 1 repeals s.1(5) of the *Immigration Act*, 1971, taking away an important guarantee that Commonwealth citizens resident in

Britain were given earlier. Section 1(5) was the only protection given in the 1971 Act to the wives and children of Commonwealth citizens who were settled in this country on 1 January 1973 when the *Immigration Act* 1971 came into force. Section 1(5) was originally enacted to give confidence to Commonwealth citizens settled here that increasingly restrictive immigration policies were not aimed at driving them away or preventing their families joining them in the UK. It also meant that those falling within it did not have to satisfy stringent maintenance and accommodation provisions as a further hurdle to family reunion (Blake and Scannell 1988:2). Thus, as the authors explain, a man who had lived and worked in this country since his arrival from Bangladesh in 1968 could be joined by his family even if he had been made redundant and was therefore in receipt of supplementary benefit. After the repeal of section 1(5) of the *Immigration Act*, 1971, however, he would have great difficulty in bringing his family over because he would most probably be unable to maintain and accommodate them without recourse to public funds. This is in no sense a 'limited' change, as claimed by the Minister, and will in practice amount to indirect discrimination.

The 1988 Act also affected the rights of polygamously married persons. David Pearl (1986:39-52) provides a fairly comprehensive summary of the law on polygamy as it stood in 1986 and its immigration consequences then. Section 2 of the 1988 Act now prevents a polygamously married woman, even if she has the right of abode in the UK, from exercising her right and settling here with her husband if another wife has preceded her. This measure, whilst affecting relatively few people [it has been estimated that about 70 such wives were admitted per year earlier on], is an example of the extent to which the Government is willing to go to reduce immigration numbers.

Section 3 requires all persons claiming the right of abode to establish this right by means of a passport describing them as British citizens, or by a certificate of entitlement. Section 5 of the 1988 Act takes away the right of appeal against a decision taken under section 3(5)(a) (breach of limited leave) or 3(5)(c) of the *Immigration Act*, 1971, to make a deportation order against a person unless he or she has been in the UK for more than seven years. No justification has been offered by the Home Office for this excessively authoritarian measure, which removes one of the most important rights of appeal given in the 1971 Act. This measure is a step backwards, given that important decisions affecting individual liberty, taken by the Government, should be subject to an appeal on its merits (for further details see Blake and Scannell 1988:2-4).

At the present moment it is too early to accurately forecast the immigration implications of the planned abolition of internal border controls within the EEC after 1st January 1993, since Britain remains opposed to this. But an issue that is currently engaging many minds is certainly the position of '1997', i.e. the rights of the British passport holders in Hong Kong (see Menski 1993). It is obviously beyond the scope of the present study to consider this issue in any depth, but it appears that the tone of the debate on Hong Kong indicates clearly that any form of non-white immigration to Britain continues to be perceived as threatening. In this context, it would seem that the question is not one of how many families from Hong Kong can be accommodated, but whether any should be accommodated at all. In other words, the reluctance, if not hostility, shown to earlier immigrants to Britain, as I showed throughout this chapter, is still evident in 1992.

While the period from the early 1970s to the present has seen a greater sophistication and manipulation of entry clearance procedures as the prime method of control, and one of its many advantages from the official perspective was that it shifted the daily administration of control overseas, and thus out of the glare of publicity, the Hong Kong debate, and the more recent discussions about asylum seekers, have brought immigration back onto the public agenda. This has also served to highlight the differential treatment of the various categories of immigrants. As we shall see in the next chapter, this differential treatment manifests itself, possibly at its most extreme, in the application of the marriage rules, with the central concern being the primary purpose rule.

The impact of new waves of immigration has at times helped the government to focus attention away from the primary purpose rule. While I was originally researching the material for this study in April 1990, Roy Hattersley MP, in a televised Parliamentary debate on the *British Nationality (Hong Kong) Bill*, made exactly this point when comparing the clearly preferential treatment being planned for a selected few families in Hong Kong, while, as he put it,

> 'If a Sikh woman from my constituency, Sikh and British, marries a man from the Punjab, that man will be subject to a searching examination of his motives and intentions if he applies to come to this country. If he says that he wants to come to Britain, in part, because he is uncertain about the future of the Punjab, he will be automatically denied entry into this country according to the 'primary purpose rule'. Anxiety about the future is a qualification for coming here if you live in Hong Kong. If you are a husband wishing to join a British wife, anxiety about the future of your country of origin anywhere else is an automatic disqualification'.

While I am not saying that the plight of many Hong Kong people, or the anxieties of so many asylum seekers, should weigh less than the concerns of spouses seeking to settle permanently in Britain, there can be no doubt that the harshness of the p.p.r. is probably not matched by any other British immigration rule. It is now time to turn to this rule itself and its gradual development into a sophisticated mechanism for the exclusion of non-white spouses of British citizens.

Chapter 3:

Origins and development of the primary purpose rule

Most of the recent leading textbooks on immigration law generally, as well as specific articles on the p.p.r., do not cover much detail on the development of the rule itself. What has been seen as 'a sordid episode in immigration history' (Bevan 1986:254) has not inspired writers to produce a detailed account of how the 'chequered history' (Bevan 1986:246) of the rules on the admission of husbands and fiancés has gradually developed. The most detailed coverage is probably found in Bhabha et al. (1985:48-76); the study by Evans (1983:131-142) as well as an article by Marrington (1985) proved useful for many details. Evans helpfully emphasises the underlying policy issues, but does not provide sufficient detail on many points that are covered or at least indicated elsewhere. More recent studies are quite vague about the early beginnings of the rule. The current editions of practice handbooks, in particular, focus on the most recent decisions and leading dicta, giving us very limited information about the genesis of the primary purpose rule. According to Ian Macdonald (1987:233):

> 'The primary purpose rule has formed part of the Immigration Rules affecting husbands since 1979 but has only become significant since 1983.'

A similar statement is found in the most recent edition of Macdonald's text (Macdonald and Blake 1991:260), while Cotran et al. (1991) took a policy decision to restrict their comments to the absolute minimum and do not refer to the history of the primary purpose rule at all. But much needs to be said about the period before 1979 to place the development of the p.p.r. into a wider context.

Since the purpose of most writing on British immigration law tends to be to provide busy practitioners with the latest detail of legal development, studies like the one produced by Dummett and Nicol (1990) are rare and, because they cover so many different issues, may not provide much detail about a specific topic such as the gradual development of the primary purpose rule.

The present chapter, therefore, outlines and analyses in detail how the p.p.r. has gradually developed, from quite liberal early provisions and a narrow statutory base in the *Immigration Act*, 1971 and even earlier legislation, into a complex and highly efficient, if not precisely equitable and just, system of exclusionary mechanisms, comprising today a substantive body of case-law, to which new cases are added practically every day. The whole of the law on primary purpose, which has probably generated more anger and anguish than any other aspect of British immigration law (Macdonald and Blake 1991:261) could be seen as amounting to a broad-based and sustained attack on continued immigration to Britain by non-white people, and those from the Indian sub-continent, in particular.

The previous chapter has already shown how, in the process of development of British immigration law as a whole, a gradual focus developed, first on non-white Commonwealth immigration generally, then on specific groups of potential immigrants, among whom spouses from the Indian subcontinent are now, undoubtedly, the most prominent category. This appears to be the case because South Asian men, in particular, have been seen as primary immigrants and have therefore been specifically targeted by the British immigration control system (Bevan 1986:246). Bhabha et al.(1985:48) have emphasised that South Asian men bore the brunt of the agitation by the anti-immigration lobby because they arrived later than the Afro-Caribbeans.

■ 3.1 The position prior to the Immigration Act, 1971

As indicated above (p.25), British immigration law and policy, once primary immigration had come under firm control, could concentrate on secondary immigration, i.e. the settlement of family members, to achieve a further reduction in numbers. Evans (1983:19-20) and Bhabha et al.(1985:48-49) show how this was sought to be achieved by restrictions on the settlement rights of spouses, children and other dependents from as early as 1969, but there seems to be evidence of earlier attempts to control numbers. Ranjit Sondhi (1987:10) has perceptively emphasised that:

> 'As the family-building process started first among West Indians and then among Indians and Pakistanis, resentment and hostility directed towards black people shifted its focus from the industrial to the social sphere. As the thought of Britain becoming a multi-racial society first struck the minds of both public and politicians alike, so the call for an end to the open-door immigration policy grew.'

Local evidence of growing hostility to Asian neighbours is, for example, documented in one of the early studies on Panjabi migrants in Britain (see Aurora 1967:35 and 91); many more examples could be given. The resulting public pressures on some politicians have been indicated already; the official legal consequences in terms of stricter immigration policies have already been discussed in chapter 2 above.

With specific reference to family reunion, Sondhi (1987:10) reports how already in May 1962, under the *Commonwealth Immigrants Act* of 1962, instructions (HMSO Cmnd 1716) were issued to immigration officers to help define dependents and to set out rules governing their entry to the UK. While the *Commonwealth Immigrants Act*, 1962 had begun to curtail primary immigration, it preserved an unequivocal right of entry for dependent relatives of workers resident in the UK. The new law worked on the then prevalent concept that women were dependent on men; the rules were, thus, very liberal when it came to the admission of female spouses, even to join a husband who was present in the UK only for a temporary purpose.

Thus, the instructions made special provisions for women who were Commonwealth citizens and could show that they were the wife of a Commonwealth citizen resident in the UK. Provided such a woman was not herself subject to a deportation order, she was to be admitted. A female Commonwealth citizen who was the wife of an alien had no such absolute right, but was to be admitted as well (Sondhi 1987:10).

The fairly considerate approach at this time is particularly illustrated by the position taken towards unmarried cohabitation, which was and is of course a prominent feature among Afro-Caribbeans, but can arise as an issue among Muslims and Hindus where there is no documentary evidence of the alleged marriage and one then applies the well-known device of presumption of marriage. It needs to be emphasised in this context that most South Asian women who sought leave to enter the UK for settlement had probably very little documentary evidence of their marital status, given that most South Asian marriages are even today not formally registered (see Menski 1988). At this early time, it appears, questioning the validity of a particular marriage as a preliminary issue, which later becomes almost an obsession of those administering the British entry clearance system, did not pose many problems. Fiancées, too, had a clearly established right of entry.

On the attempt to understand and respect local custom and different legal traditions, Sondhi (1987:10) reports:

> 'A woman living in permanent association with a Commonwealth citizen was to be treated as a wife and immigration officers were told to bear in mind any local custom or tradition in establishing the permanence of the association.'

The potential difficulties for South Asian spouses are not even alluded to here by Sondhi; presumably this was not a big issue at the time, as discretion was exercised in the applicant's favour. Other writers, too, e.g., Bevan (1986:244) indicate much more readiness than we would witness today in recognising the importance of overseas customs and traditions (on which see now in detail Powell 1991 and 1992).

A clearly less liberal, but similarly considerate approach was taken to the admission of husbands. The instructions stated that, apart from special cases which might justify refusal,

'The normal rule should be to treat a Commonwealth citizen as eligible for admission if the Immigration Officer is satisfied that he is coming to join his wife and the latter is ordinarily resident in the United Kingdom' (HMSO, Cmnd 1716, para 29).

On this, Sondhi (1987:11) reports that a Commonwealth citizen husband coming to join a wife who was ordinarily resident in the UK was to be admitted, unless there was no reasonable prospect of his maintaining himself or his family without recourse to public funds. This is significant evidence of the early existence of maintenance requirements, but the test applied at this early stage appears to have been fairly lenient. In doubtful cases, apparently, the immigration officer in his or her discretion was to consider the strength of the wife's connection with the UK, including length of residence. It may be assumed that this particular provision could be satisfied more easily by white women who had lived in Britain throughout than by women who were recent immigrants and might be non-white, but there are no indications that the instructions of 1962 caused widespread hardship.

The argument of strength of the wife's connection with the UK is, of course, a line of reasoning that should also be useful today when one considers the position of British-born Asian women seeking to be joined in the UK by a husband from South Asia, or indeed from anywhere in the world.

Sondhi (1987:11) has concluded that these early rules were 'liberal indeed' compared with those that followed later. He shows how the official discussion of immigration during the mid-1960s gradually turned to the argument of reducing not only the numbers of people entering on work vouchers, but also to curtailing the entry of dependents.

The position regarding family reunion remained unchanged even after the passing of the *Commonwealth Immigrants Act* of 1968. It would appear that concern about the mass entry of East African Asians (see Steel 1969) topped the agenda then, rather than the entry of spouses from the subcontinent. Nevertheless, the racist underpinnings of the 1968 Act were, in due course, to have effects on the entry rights of New Commonwealth spouses.

Indeed, it did not take long till the accusation of widespread abuse and evasion of immigration control by making false claims gained in popularity as a major justification for tightening control mechanisms for certain categories of people. This method of justifying further restrictions appears to be a popular and efficient device used by politicians, then as now. Indications that the identity of dependents and the validity of their claims would be more thoroughly scrutinised were at first aimed particularly at children and dependent parents (see Sondhi 1987:11-12; Bhabha et al. 1985:48; see in detail Dummett 1973). These agonising developments led, ultimately, to the introduction of important new appeals procedures, with which we are not centrally concerned here.

Recently, Dummett and Nicol (1990:206-207) have documented in some detail that the early restrictions against Commonwealth husbands were based on statistics that showed, for example, that in 1968 a total of 1676 Commonwealth citizens were admitted to the UK as spouses joining a woman resident in the UK. We do not know how many of these men were of South Asian origin, but their total number is almost half that of the 3828 males admitted in the same year under the employment voucher scheme. James Callaghan, as Dummett and Nicol (1990:206) quote, argued the case for control, saying that,

'It seems marriage is being used by many young men of working age as a means of entering, working and settling in this country. This abuse of the concession is inconsistent with the general scheme of Commonwealth immigration control.'·

Since the admission of such men had so far taken place under a discretionary provision, it was very easy to take that discretion away. Thus, without any change in the statute law and with immediate effect from 30th January 1969, instructions were issued to immigration officers to restrict the admission of husbands and fiancés from the Commonwealth 'to cases presenting special features' (HMSO, Cmnd. 4298 [1970], quoted in Dummett and Nicol 1990:206). It was also laid down that henceforth such applicants needed to have an entry certificate prior to setting out for the UK, and a separate set of instructions put restrictions on men who were already in the UK, whether as visitors, students or for other temporary purposes. They, too, except in exceptional circumstances, would not be permitted to settle in the UK on the basis of their marriage.

These restrictive instructions were then formalised in the *Immigration Appeals Act* of 1969, which not only introduced a system of appeals, but also made the holding of an entry certificate mandatory. Despite some protests, this was pushed through and the new rules were also supplemented by fresh instructions to immigration officers 'to limit the admission of husbands and fiancés to cases where there were special considerations that made exclusion 'undesirable'' (Sondhi 1987:13). Indeed, the position now was that alien husbands and fiancés were in a more favourable position than Commonwealth citizens (Sondhi 1987:13; Dummett and Nicol 1990: 207).

It has been argued that these new instructions formally institutionalised sex discrimination in British immigration control (Marrington 1985:537). Evans (1983:19) has pointed out without much further comment that 'in 1969 a woman settled in the United Kingdom ceased to be permitted to be joined by her husband'. In a sense, this was a logical consequence of the lenient approach to the entry rights of women, since English law at that time still saw women primarily as dependents. Various authors have taken it virtually as an established fact that, 'in the UK, a sharp distinction has been drawn between the rights of women and men' (Bevan 1986:243). More recently, Macdonald and Blake (1991: 243) have stated clearly that some of the old sex discrimination against women still lingers on in British immigration law and that traditional role models are still the operative assumption in many situations. It is not surprising, then, that the main victims of the increasingly strict entry clearance requirements for spouses would, at least *prima facie*, be men, while the rights of women to family life received less attention, though the material test at the time was whether exclusion of the husband would cause hardship to the wife.

Bhabha et al. (1985:48-49) have collected material to show that those in charge of immigration policy at the time purported to be well aware of social problems created by the refusal of women and children to join men already settled in the UK. Their analysis accordingly seeks to explain the genesis of the ban on the entry of New Commonwealth husbands in a different way by emphasising another relevant point, namely that white men's fears of 'wifeless' black men overrode other concerns and that, therefore, women and children continued to be admitted as dependents, albeit with stricter controls which, as we know, ultimately led to a huge controversy about the 'not related as claimed' insinuations, which have then created such an important role for the DNA technique in immigration law.

By retaining the right for men to bring in dependents while abolishing it for women, as Bhabha et al. (1985:49) argue, the government in reality preserved the right of white men to bring to the UK any spouse of their choice. This policy would still allow those in charge of immigration control to circumscribe and qualify the rights of certain dependents, namely those from New Commonwealth countries, where the sponsor was himself originally from overseas. Thus, even though far fewer husbands than wives came to Britain each year (Bhabha et al. 1985:49), the strategy, in 1969, to prevent women from bringing in husbands from abroad achieved multiple goals: the primary policy aim of reducing the number of New Commonwealth immigrants was coupled with preserving male superiority generally and protecting the white male's ego from too intense 'coloured' competition for women.

The new rule, it must be emphasised, deprived all women settled in Britain of a right that they had previously enjoyed, albeit at the discretion of immigration officers. Yet while the introduction of this new rule was deceptively simple, its actual application had to run into difficulties sooner or later, since *prima facie* it applied to every woman, irrespective of ethnic background.

Apparently, it took a while till it was fully realised that the 1969 rule was a blatant case of sexual discrimination which did little credit to the UK, though it seemed, then, to be supported by European law, on grounds that the women were not barred from marriage and had a choice between staying in the UK or joining their partners abroad (*Papayianni* [1974] Imm AR 7), unlike the East African Asian cases where the dependents had nowhere else to go (for details see Bevan 1986:247).

Initially, much energy was spent on defining in what 'special circumstances' discretion could still be exercised in the male applicant's favour. Bevan (1986:247) reports on 'a sordid succession of cases assessing the degree of hardship' caused to women. Marrington (1985:538) reports that:

'In practice, the hardship proviso proved to be a formidable obstacle to family life, particularly as it was interpreted by the Immigration Appeal Tribunal to mean serious and lasting harm.'

There are indications that also some English women who had married foreign men were caught up in this rule. This, it appears, finally led to attempts to abolish the offensive rule by a Private Member's Bill in 1974 (see Bevan 1986:266, note 53; Marrington 1985:538 and further below).

Several writers (Dummett and Nicol 1990:207; Bhabha et al. 1985:49; Evans 1983:19-20) have correctly emphasised that these new rules had the explicit purpose and effect to refuse men from the Indian subcontinent, while applicants from elsewhere faced far less difficulty. One can probably argue that with the beginning of restrictions against the right of entry to the UK even of certain British citizens in the *Commonwealth Immigrants Act* of 1968, not only public opinion and the political climate, but also the legal structures had now moved towards harsh restrictions against the entry of spouses from certain backgrounds. The emergence of the criterion of a close connection with the UK in the *Commonwealth Immigrants Act* of 1968, not simply the now increasingly meaningless Commonwealth link, made the claim of Commonwealth citizen spouses that little bit more tenuous and gave them a lesser standing in a competitive environment.

It seems quite apparent, then, that a combination of socio-cultural and economic arguments underpins the beginnings of the immigration restrictions focused against Commonwealth spouses, leading to the curtailing of women's rights through restrictions on the entry rights of men. Within a few years, between 1962 and 1969, a humane and considerate, if sexually biased, policy on the admission of spouses had been replaced by a potentially and actually tight restriction — in effect, almost a total ban — on the entry of male spouses from certain parts of the Commonwealth. In theory, of course, this could hit white Australians as much as South Asians, but it clearly did not do this, just as much as the current application of the p.p.r. does not affect white Americans or Australians (Macdonald 1987:233-234).

In practice, as Bhabha et al (1985:50-51) have shown, with several examples, the 1969 restrictions meant that:

> 'The only women who had any chance of bringing in foreign-born husbands were white women who would have to live in a country without a large European population in order to be with their husbands.'

In particular, racist and sexist assumptions of the roles of Asian women, and of women in society generally, led to immigration decisions that expected women to join their husband, wherever he was settled, i.e. to follow the traditional patrilocal/virilocal model. These assumptions hit not only some white women, but in particular young Asians who had grown up in Britain. This point is of utmost relevance today, since the number of such young Asian women today is much larger, and the same traditional stereotypes and expectations are still being used to justify the refusal of claims by British Asian women that they should be allowed to bring their South Asian husbands to Britain, where their jobs and homes are, and where many of them have lived since birth.

It has rightly been pointed out that here is a hidden agenda of repatriation strategies, since expecting Asian women to settle with their husbands in South Asia, or anywhere else in the world except Britain, has exactly that effect (see e.g. Bhabha et al. 1985:51). Then, as now, the concept that 'they' should go 'home', where 'they' properly belonged, can be shown to be a powerful notion that evokes strong emotions.

The examples of cases referred to by Bhabha et al. (1985:50-51) clearly show that European women marrying South Asian men might have a chance to be joined by their husbands in Britain but Asian women in the same situation would not. This may have been an added reason why a significant number of South Asian men married European women during the 1960s and early 1970s, a trend that is now, under the long-term effects of the primary purpose rule, reversed to the extent that an increasing number of Asian women in Britain is marrying European men.

Human rights concerns and equal opportunities objections notwithstanding, to relax the restrictions of the 1969 rules would of course have meant increasing male immigration to the UK, though no one appears to have been able to put reliable figures on the extent of the 'problem' (Bevan 1986:247). While the sensitive changes in the new *Immigration Act* of 1971 were being debated, nothing changed regarding the position of spouses. As we shall see further below, however, the restrictions of 1969 had to be relaxed in 1974, at least for some time, only to be tightened again later. This clearly shows how British immigration policy has desperately vacillated between upholding basic human rights and preventing the entry of more people from the New Commonwealth.

■ 3.2 The role of the Immigration Act, 1971

In view of the dilemma created by the 1969 rules, discussed immediately above, it comes as no surprise that this otherwise important Act does not really tell us anything about the primary purpose rule at all. As so often in immigration law, dry legal language carefully papers over the real socio-cultural concerns. Section 3(2) of the Act merely states:

> 'The Secretary of State shall from time to time (and as soon as may be) lay before Parliament statements of the rules, or of any changes in the rules, laid down by him as to practice to be followed in the administration of this Act for regulating the entry into and stay in the United Kingdom of persons required by this Act to have leave to enter, including any rules as to the period for which leave is to be given and the conditions to be attached in different circumstances; and section 1(4) above shall not be taken to require uniform provision to be made by the rules as regards admission of persons for a purpose or in a capacity specified in section 1(4)....'

Section 1(4) of the 1971 Act provides as follows:

> 'The rules laid down by the Secretary of State as to the practice to be followed in the administration of this Act for regulating the entry into and stay in the United Kingdom of persons not having the right of abode shall include provision for admitting (in such cases and subject to such restrictions as may be provided by the rules, and subject or not to conditions as to length of stay or otherwise) persons coming for the purpose of taking employment, or for purposes of study, or as visitors, or as dependents of persons lawfully in or entering the United Kingdom.'

It will be noted that spouses are not even explicitly mentioned here, which may well mean that by 1971 those in charge of phrasing the new law were desperately concerned not to raise contested issues and to avoid drawing attention to the existing powers to make 'better' rules for the entry of spouses.

The above-cited two sections together provide the statutory basis for the authority and wide discretion given to the Secretary of State for the Home Office in formulating the substantive body of British immigration law, which is found in a constantly modified set of Immigration Rules which, as Vincenzi and Marrington (1992:v) emphasise, not only 'fleshes out' the rather rudimentary and skeletal structure of the Act itself, but actually forms the substantive basis for British immigration decisions at all levels. Since the introduction of the 1971 Act, as we have seen in chapter 2.5 already, there have been many revisions of the Rules. This illustrates the importance of section 3(2) of the 1971 Act in the development of British immigration law in principle, while in practice, as Vincenzi and Marrington (1992) now remind us so forcefully, we have to look to the various sets of Immigration Rules to ascertain how the entry rights of spouses have been regulated since 1971.

■ 3.3 The rules between 1974 and 1977: Balancing immigration consequences and hardship

We have already seen in chapter 3.1 above that the tight restrictions on the entry rights of husbands, especially those from the New Commonwealth, began to cause dismay soon after 1969. By 1974, apparently a year of commitment to equality in British law-making, 'the pressure for reform had become politically irresistible' (Marrington 1985:538), as cases of British women separated from their husbands under the 1969 rules mounted, and local M.P.s began to demand relief for their constituents from the Labour government of the day.

As a result of widespread publicity and pressure, and the embarrassing appearance of a Private Member's Bill, the *Spouses of UK Citizens (Equal Treatment) Bill* of 1974, the newly-elected Labour government finally reconsidered the legal position on the admission of male spouses and fiancés in 1974. In March 1974, Lord Fenner Brockway's request in the House of Lords that there should be equality of treatment for men and women in the marriage rules was still rebuked by a simplistic reference to the 'floodgates' argument and the need to promote racial harmony by exercising strict immigration controls (Bhabha et al. 1985:52). In the House of Commons, Lena Jeger M.P., the sponsor of the Private Member's Bill, pointed to the large numbers of British women caught up in this discriminatory system (for details see Bhabha et al. 1985:52) and brought about a public debate on the issue, emphasising that it was not exclusively a South Asian problem, but made life difficult for many white women. There were newspaper stories about the plight of British women married to foreign academics (see Bhabha et al. 1985:56), and the more favourable position of women covered by the provisions of ECC law was emphasised (Evans 1983:131).

It is interesting and relevant to note here that the focus of concern at this time was not on 'coloured' men from the New Commonwealth, but on white women, whose right to bring a husband or fiancé to Britain was being impaired. Similarly, more recently, calls for the abolition of the primary purpose rule have been supported by the argument that British men — which really meant 'white' men — should be able to bring in spouses or fiancées from anywhere in the world. This argument, it needs to be emphasised, grew after the refusal of a number of applications by Filipino and Thai women to join their partners in the UK. Here again, the numbers are small, but the concerns of a few white people in Britain appear to receive more prominence than those of many more non-white individuals caught up in entry clearance cases.

Regarding the debate in 1974, we have a telling comment by Roy Jenkins, the then Home Secretary, who at first would not contemplate any relaxation of the immigration rules, but then appears to have applied his mind to the question and found that he was not impressed, on mature consideration (Bevan 1986:247), with the alleged abuses of immigration control nor, significantly, with the argument of numbers:

'When I first considered this I believe that I put too high the likely immigration consequences and did not fully allow for the stark and unacceptable nature of the discrimination. On further consideration of all the issues involved in this difficult problem, I am persuaded that there are no sufficiently compelling reasons for denying the parties to the marriage the freedom of choice that I believe they should have.' (H.C. Debates, cols.535-536 [27th June 1974], quoted by Marrington 1985:538).

Thus, on 27th June 1974, new instructions were announced and issued (*H.C. Debates* [27 June 1974, col.535), followed by new Rules in August (HMSO: Cmnd 5715-18 [1974]), while the Private Member's Bill was withdrawn. This had the effect that discrimination on the basis of sex was, at least officially, eliminated from British immigration control by the new Rules. Henceforth, fiancés and husbands would be able to join their female partners in the UK. Husbands, regardless of their nationality, could join their wives in Britain, provided that the woman had settled status, whereas fiancés would be admitted for three months in the first instance. In other immigration situations, however, as Bhabha et al. (1985:53) show, full equality between women and men was never achieved.

But it does not surprise that a system of more or less open entry as a spouse to a country that otherwise operated strict immigration controls against non-white persons had to face challenges more or less immediately. True, the aspect of gender discrimination had been settled more or less satisfactorily, but the racial and cultural dimensions of the immigration consequences of the new rules did not let the opposition rest for a moment. As early as December 1974, David Lane, a conservative M.P. who subsequently became the Chairman of the Commission for Racial Equality, asked the then Home Secretary:

'What safeguards are now operating to prevent abuse of the Immigration Rules governing entry of men or women to join spouses settled in the United Kingdom?' (Hansard, 3rd December 1974).

Thus, as happened in 1969, allegations of abuse were raised to justify a retreat from the liberal provisions of the 1974 Rules. While there was some evidence of an increase in the numbers of persons seeking entry to the UK as spouses (Evans 1983:133 provides a table of statistics), including of course many non-white persons, it was clearly not only the numbers issue that was emphasised, but also the familiar threat of Britain being 'swamped' by people from far-flung lands that had nothing but a nominal historical connection with the UK.

The ground for reform was prepared in what appears to be a concerted effort of scaremongering and raising racist undertones. Bhabha et al. (1985:54-55) have reported in some detail how in Parliament, especially during 1976, concern was voiced about the changing demographic nature of Britain in terms of the outflow of young white people and the influx of young persons from the New Commonwealth. In a Parliamentary Debate on 24th May 1976, William Whitelaw, then the Opposition Spokesman on Home Affairs, criticised the new liberal regime as dangerous in view of long-term immigration implications, since, as he put it:

> 'Girls and boys in this country can seek a partner of their own ethnic group from the country from where their parents originally came... a process which could go on for ever.' (Hansard, 24th May 1976).

Not surprisingly, Enoch Powell, in the same debate, disclosing the existence of a confidential Foreign Office document, the so-called 'Hawley Report', went much further. This report on the entry clearance system in the Indian subcontinent expressed concern about the 'multiplier effect' of allowing entry to husbands and fiancés, as it would subsequently entitle 'parents, grandparents and allegedly distressed relatives of the fiancé to apply' (Hansard, 24th May 1976). This, in turn, was lapped up by the press, which indulged in reporting Powell's warnings of inner-city violence as a result of the continuing entry of relatives from the Indian subcontinent (for details see Bhabha et al. 1985:54).

Significantly, the commitment to equal treatment of males and females in immigration law was challenged by another male M.P. on the ground that allowing men to move to the place of settlement of their wives was 'contrary to the way of life of the people concerned', both in Britain and in the subcontinent (see Bhabha et al. 1985:55). This argument was, of course, diametrically opposed to the one used by Lena Jeger M.P. when she sought to introduce her Private Member's Bill, namely that women should have equal rights in immigration matters and should not be automatically expected to live in the place of their husband 'as part of his baggage.' (see Bhabha et al. 1985:52).

Here, then, we find an indication of the alleged abuse of custom by South Asian spouses, who are expected to follow the patrilocal model of residence, so that the bride should move to the husband's home after marriage, and not vice versa. This argument, coupled with widespread allegations about 'bogus' marriages and the ubiquitous reference to the mistakenly allowed increase in immigration by the 1974 relaxation, seems to have had some effect.

Gradually, the government formed a view that the new liberal system of entry clearance for men was being abused and had unacceptable immigration implications. This change of attitude was assisted by the inability to provide reliable statistics, which abets and facilitates scaremongering. It was also, as Bevan (1986:247) found,

> 'Fuelled by lurid and extravagant press claims of illegal immigration racketeering, a trade in forged documents and 'brides for purchase.''

Thus, by March 1977, Britain retreated from its attempt to operate a non-discriminatory system of immigration control for spouses and began to re-introduce stricter conditions which had the double effect of reducing the numbers of entry clearances granted to applicants and of introducing new but not necessarily subtler forms of discrimination. The tightening up process operated, in the main, through the use of the notion of 'marriages of convenience'. We shall see below how this was done, and that it proved to be an approach that was not efficient enough to control numbers. Thus, further steps, ultimately the development of the primary purpose rule itself, had to be taken. The concept of marriage of convenience is, therefore, an intermediary stage in the development of the full-blown conceptual disaster of the primary purpose rule.

■ 3.4 Marriages of convenience and immigration law

The concept of a marriage of convenience, i.e. arranging a legal marriage that is not, in fact, a genuine marital union, just to be able to obtain some specific benefits, is also known as 'sham marriage' and has first of all given rise to the question whether such a marriage should be regarded as a nullity. Bromley (1981:91-92) briefly discussed this question, anticipating that this problem:

> 'may become more important in these days of political, racial and religious persecution and restricted immigration when, for example, a woman who is a citizen of state X may go through a form of marriage with a citizen of state Y merely in order to escape from X or to enter Y on the strength of her husband's nationality or passport.' (Bromley 1981:92).

Bromley (1981:92) also refers to some earlier cases on the legal validity of sham marriages. Several reported cases regarding marriages of convenience after the Second World War, mostly involving alien women seeking to settle in Britain (for details see Macdonald 1987:228), confirm that the concept itself was well-known in the 1970s. Such marriages continue to be valid marriages in English law, 'whatever the purposes of the parties' (Macdonald 1987:228; Macdonald and Blake 1991:257). This position was reaffirmed by the House of Lords in *Vervaeke* v. *Smith* ([1983] AC 145, [1982] All ER 144) and had been accepted before in a number of cases (cited by Macdonald and Blake 1991:257 n.1), even where the marriage had been contracted with the object of evading or circumventing immigration control, though there is some disquiet about such arrangements (see Bevan 1986:266 n.61 with reference to adoptions).

But, as Macdonald emphasises in the second edition of his handbook (1987:228), while the third edition carries a much-reduced coverage of this topic (Macdonald and Blake 1991:257-258), a marriage of convenience does not nowadays confer any immigration rights on a spouse.

A reference to 'marriages of convenience' was apparently first introduced into British immigration parlance in 1970 with regard to aliens by Cmnd 4296 (Aliens — Instructions to Immigration Officers, para 43), as laid before Parliament in February 1970:

> 'An alien married to a British subject may be admitted to join his wife in the United Kingdom if: (a) she was born in the UK and has since lived here, or (b) she has, at least, substantial connections with this country and is well-established here, provided... the Immigration Officer is satisfied that the marriage is not one of convenience, entered into to obtain a lodgement here.' (for details see Marrington 1985:537).

The above excerpt illustrates and confirms that at this time the motive of an 'international' marriage was becoming an issue looked at more seriously in terms of immigration implications. Since there was, as we saw already, official awareness as early as 1968 that husbands from certain countries might seek to marry a woman resident in Britain to be able to settle here, the term 'marriage of convenience' began to be used more frequently and could now be employed to reject the claims of British women that they should be allowed to live in Britain with their foreign husbands. But the concept never really played a prominent role in public debates till 1976. Also, quite apparently, the notion of the 'primary purpose' of a marriage is a later distinction of some sophistication.

The importance of the above-cited instructions lies, to a certain extent, also in the mere fact of their existence. When one is, a few years later, confronted with what appears to be a totally new and unjust rule, in the form of the p.p.r., it could always be argued by the advocates of strict immigration control that the p.p.r. was not, in fact, anything new, nor was it contrived to meet the whims and wishes of those who formulated the Rules, but it was actually a reiteration of a policy firmly seated in the administrative arsenal of immigration law much earlier. The strict application of the new rule could then simply be justified by further allegations of widespread abuse and the need to control or keep down numbers.

Bromley's example, cited above, and most of the case-law, still concerned women in cases of marriages of convenience, but the emphasis gradually shifted to men. The notion that many foreign men would readily arrange a marriage with a British-settled woman only to be able to live in Britain clearly came into great prominence during the immigration debates in 1976 (see e.g. Marrington 1985:538). It is, of course, flattering to think that one's country is a desirable place to live in, but it would clearly seem to matter who wished to come for settlement: while more non-white men applied for settlement in Britain, as we have already seen, there was evidence that many young white British people turned their backs on the country. So the objections to male immigration after the rule changes in 1974 were in reality a matter of apprehensions about non-white immigration.

It appears that the allegation of widespread abuse of the British immigration rules by men from South Asia was used as a lever to force rule changes as soon as the liberal rules of 1974 had been passed. This then sparked off a desperate search for legal means to control the alleged new 'flood' of male immigrants. This, in turn, led first to some restrictions on the entry of men to Britain in 1977, in particular the introduction of probationary periods, which have become a permanent feature of the Immigration Rules since then and have been heavily criticised (see e.g. Bevan 1986:247-248). Only a few years later do we see the introduction of the primary purpose rule itself, which developed out of the notion of 'marriage of convenience'.

However, the notion that men can easily arrange bogus marriages to be able to come to Britain is far too simplistic, typically male-centred, and underrates the importance placed in many cultures on the permanency of a marital union and the concern for the continued happiness of one's daughter or sister. One of the most experienced British family reunion lawyers, Nuala Mole (1987:29), has forcefully and very appropriately argued against the notion of bogus immigration marriages among Asians in the context of arranged marriages:

> 'It is important also for advisers to understand that ECOs and Home Office officials are still largely drawn from a white majority culture who find it difficult not to see arranged marriages as the forcing of unwilling girls into unloving liaisons with men who perceive them only as chattels. In reality the vast majority of marriages are arranged with a view to ensuring the continued happiness of a much loved child and to maintaining or improving the status of the family within their community. Crucial to this end is that the union should be successful and be seen to be so in the eyes of both extended families.'

Prior to 1977, marriages of convenience for both men and women could lead to discretionary refusals under the general provisions of the Immigration Rules (see Control after Entry — Commonwealth, 1973, H.C. 80, para 4; see also *Vasilejevic* [1976] Imm AR 44 and *Nathvani* [1979-80] Imm AR 9 QBD). However, it appears that this discretion to refuse immigration rights was in practice hardly ever used against women, who had also better rights as dependents under the *Immigration Act* of 1971, particularly section 1(5), and under EEC law. But it is quite apparent that the power to refuse entry clearance was increasingly used against South Asian men during the 1970s and 1980s, particularly after the rule changes in 1977.

The Immigration Rules of 1977 (HC 238-241), with effect from 22nd March 1977, included for the first time a reference to 'primary purpose'. They laid down that an entry clearance would be refused,

> '...if the officer to whom the application is made has reason to believe that the proposed marriage would be one of convenience entered into primarily to obtain admission here with no intention that the parties should live together permanently as man and wife.'

Marrington, writing that British immigration law here 'lurched once more into a period of discrimination, encapsulated in the notion of 'primary purpose'' (1985:538) tells us not only that this formal amendment of the Immigration Rules reflected restrictive practices that had already been followed by officers investigating suspected marriages of convenience. He also argues that the formal introduction of the convenience proviso helped to avoid stating the real issue, namely that it was now no longer perceived as conducive to the public good that so many non-white men should enter Britain as spouses or fiancés. The rules about marriages of convenience,

> 'enabled officers to refuse applications on that specific ground rather than on the more nebulous, and perhaps politically sensitive, ground that the presence of such applicants in the United Kingdom was not conducive to the public good.' (Marrington 1985:538).

It is also important to point out here specifically the use of the wording 'reason to believe', since this introduced an element of subjectivity in the assessment of the motives of spouses which increases their burden of proof. We shall see in the next sub-chapter that this particular issue was, in due course, to gain great importance in the government's strategy to curb numbers and to maintain the discretionary powers of immigration officials.

The new Rules again made it difficult for many women to be joined by their husband or fiancé, since only men could be required to prove the *bona fides* of their marriage, and they would have to take this hurdle twice. While the 1977 Rules shielded women from the same intrusiveness to which men were now exposed, it could, however, not be said that women were treated equally. In fact, the 1977 Rules again insinuate that when men join women, rather than the other way around, there must be some ulterior motive to the marriage. Thus, a learning process in applying intimidation and interrogation techniques was initiated, leading to the eventual fine-tuning of the notion of 'marriage of convenience' into the 'primary purpose' concept.

Evans (1983:133) gives some evidence of the consequent decline of the figures of men admitted for settlement in the UK after 1977, though the new legal rules necessarily led to statistical distortions. Evans rightly points to the fact that men who had been married less than a year would now be admitted only for a limited period, not immediately for permanent settlement, whereas, it would appear, fiancés in particular faced the risk of having their application rejected altogether. Notably, Evans argues that there cannot have been a serious problem about marriages of convenience, since between March 1977 and 30th September 1979 only 356 men were refused leave to remain indefinitely after their 12 months' probationary period (Evans 1983:133). Similarly, pressed in Parliament, a Junior Minister at the Home Office could only vaguely suggest a figure of several hundred cases, a fact which Bevan (1986:247) saw as

'... telling testimony to the power of the press, to the fickleness and expediency of Governments in immigration matters and the use of statistical imprecision.'

Apart from such critical comments, writers on the subject are extremely brief in their coverage of this particular period, which is crucial for the development of the primary purpose rule. Criticism of the 1977 Rules as a return to discriminatory practices and discretionary powers that may be overstretched is apparent; but it is only in very subtle terms indicated that the 1977 Rules were not, in fact, very effective in reducing the number of male spouses seeking to join women who were settled in the UK. Apart from providing telling statistics, as we saw above, Evans (1983:134) simply seems to say that the next set of Immigration Rules in 1980 'went further', while Sondhi (1987:15) speaks of 'even more restrictive rules' and Macdonald (1987:228) refers to 'a far more stringent test of primary purpose' since 1979.

Bhabha et al. (1985:56) rightly emphasise the fact that the 1977 restrictions 'only led to demands for more' and provide some useful details on the government's attempts to examine 'the whole question of immigration.' Not surprisingly, though, family reunion remained the focus of concerted actions to introduce a tougher regime of rules.

Technically, the 1977 Rules had made it necessary to ascertain what was meant by marriages of convenience. A marriage of convenience in immigration law, as Macdonald (1987:228) explained, consisted of two elements:

(a) that it was primarily entered into to obtain settlement;

(b) that there was no intention of living together permanently as man and wife.

Both elements had to be proved by the Home Office before the discretion to refuse admission or leave could be exercised (*Mahmud Khan* [1983] QB 790 and [1982] Imm AR 134 CA). Where settlement had already been granted to an applicant on the basis of a marriage which was then subsequently shown by the Home Office to be a marriage of convenience, the applicant became liable to deportation on grounds conducive to the public good under section 3(5)(b) of the 1971 Act. Thus, in *Cheema* ([1982] Imm AR 124 CA) the view was expressed that marriage was a fundamental institution of society which should not be threatened by false marriages for immigration purposes.

It may be difficult to argue with such a moralistic stance, but it would in practice not often be possible to find evidence that there had been a marriage of convenience unless there was evidence of a breakdown or in fact the non-existence of marital relations. If it is indeed correct that South Asian families resident in Britain had started to find husbands for their daughters and sisters from the subcontinent, there is every likelihood that such marriages would be as genuine, and as permanent, as normal South Asian marriages. It simply became a result of the growing dispersal of the South Asian diaspora all over the world that international marriage arrangements became more frequent.

An immigration policy that wanted to curtail the numbers of men entering Britain by simply ascertaining the genuineness of marriages would not, therefore, have much scope of success. In other words, the scheme of the 1977 Rules was not a realistic and efficient way of reducing the numbers of men seeking to enter Britain as spouses, since most South Asian marriages were clearly genuine marriages to whom the traditional notion of 'marriage of convenience' could not be sensibly applied.

In those few cases where a marriage could indeed be shown not to have lasted till the end of the probationary period, or where there was evidence of a bogus arrangement, the legal consequences were clear enough, so that Ian Macdonald (1987:228) is quite correct to say, though he does this with reference to the 1979 Rules, that 'where a marriage is one of convenience it will automatically fall foul of the primary purpose rule.' In other words, except possibly for those men who were thrown out by their wives during the probationary period, and may or may not be 'innocent', there would be few victims of the new regime of control, since the overwhelming majority of marriages would no doubt be genuine. To challenge their status as 'bogus marriages' was not only harmful in terms of community relations (see for example the outrage repeatedly indicated by Sondhi 1987), it was, as discussed above, in most cases impossible to sustain the insinuation or claim of fraudulent use of such marriages. So it appears that the device of seeing South Asian marriages as 'marriages of convenience' was too simplistic and could not lead to the desired results in terms of immigration policies.

This created a big dilemma, in that the policy objectives of the new Rules in terms of reduction of numbers could not be achieved by genuine means, i.e. a straightforward application of the Rules.

It is this fact which explains, above all, why the incoming Conservative government, in a mood approaching something like sheer desperation, enforced a new set of Immigration Rules that firmly institutionalised the primary purpose rule. Their introduction must be seen as indicating an admission to the effect that officially designated 'marriages of convenience' were in fact, with very few exceptions, perfectly genuine marriages.

A further dimension of controlling the entry of spouses, and male spouses in particular, is of course that of breaking the whole process of arranging international marriages over time. We already saw above (p.53) how William Whitelaw had warned, in 1976, that young Asians might go on forever importing spouses from the subcontinent. A further aim of effective immigration control procedures would therefore have to be to put people off the idea of making such arrangements in future. Surprisingly, this has not been seen as an important issue by those who wrote on the subject. In fact, Bevan (1986:243) appears to envisage only the need for men to find brides overseas, though he mentions the implications of the arranged marriage system, while other writers make no comments on this issue at all.

As we shall see, however, British immigration control procedures after 1977 increasingly and quite desperately sought to devise techniques that allow officials to reject the applications of spouses for entry or settlement, even though they are parties to genuine marriages. In this context, Macdonald (1987:228) has quite rightly indicated that the introduction of the far more stringent test of 'primary purpose' of a marriage in 1979 made the consideration of marriages of convenience of lesser relevance. Consequently, as he emphasises, under the now developing stricter regime,

'... the intention of the spouses to live together permanently as man and wife does not necessarily mean that the marriage gets over the primary purpose hurdle.'

It appears, thus, that between 1977 and 1979 those in charge of British immigration controls attempted to find a way out of the dilemma created by the ineffectiveness of the 1977 Rules about 'marriages of convenience'. The mental link between 'convenience' and 'purpose' had already been drawn. Now it became expedient to establish the concept of 'primary purpose', which did not necessarily mean that the marriage was not genuine, but rather that the marriage itself was a secondary consideration, the primary one being immigration to the UK.

■ 3.5 The formal introduction of the primary purpose rule

The previous sub-chapter has already shown how the pressure to introduce more effective restrictions on the entry and settlement rights of overseas husbands and fiancés had built up after 1974 and was not actually reduced by the 1977 Rules which attempted to weed out male applicants who were parties to a 'marriage of convenience'. We also saw that while one was aware of difficulties in ascertaining the genuineness of marriages, a more effective device to reduce the number of male applicants from South Asia was urgently needed. The easiest way to achieve this would be to restrict, again, the rights of women to sponsor a husband or fiancé for settlement in the UK. But this could only be a first step, fraught with many difficulties in view of the growing resistance to openly discriminatory rules, and the increase of rights to family life brought about by EEC law.

The present section shows in detail how, firstly, the British debate developed between 1977 and 1980 around an obsession with figures of male immigrants from South Asia, soon leading to an openly discriminatory regime of tougher immigration control, explicitly designed to hit non-white male applicants by restricting women's rights to sponsor a spouse. We shall also see how later, when the sexually discriminatory British rules are modified as a result of pressures from Europe, the primary purpose rule gains in importance as a most effective exclusionary mechanism.

The first sub-section will consider in detail how the Immigration Rules of 1980 (HC 394) came to be introduced. The second part provides relevant material and some comments on the new Rules themselves, while the third part seeks to analyse in detail how the concept of 'primary purpose' underwent intricate modifications from the early 1980s up to the present day, becoming an ever more sophisticated mechanism for the exclusion of as many non-white male spouses and fiancés as possible. The balancing act between human rights and immigration consequences continues. But the balance, it appears from the study of this crucial period, has been shifting away from genuine concern about even basic human rights to an obsession with immigration statistics. The end result, as several commentators have critically noted, is what Marrington (1985:536) has openly called an unjust system of 'discriminatory control without fear of judicial obstruction'.

☐ 3.5.1 The perceived need for tighter immigration control

In an effort to slow down the rate of entry of husbands, already in 1975 separate non-priority queues for men had been created; they simply and effectively staggered the rate of admission of husbands and fiancés. But there was no end to the queue itself, and the issue of male immigration from South Asia continued to have a high profile. Marrington (1985:538) tells us that despite the 1977 Rules,

> '... allegations of 'back door' immigration continued, and by late 1979 the *purpose* of the proposed marriage had become a distinct focus of enquiry, divorced from its earlier link with marriages of convenience and, remarkably, somewhat detached from the *intentions* of the parties.'

The introduction of a probationary period of 12 months for marriages in 1977, somewhat arbitrary in itself, could and did lead to abuses: if the marriage lasted one day longer, the husband was safe from the rule placing him on probation. However, the marriage had to subsist at the date when the Secretary of State reviewed it, not at the time when the immigrant applied to stay (Bevan 1986:247). This rule placed husbands in a position of considerable uncertainty, because their right to stay lay in suspension.

Also, since the situation of husbands on probation allowed a man's spouse to determine the extent of his stay, all one needed to 'prove' the existence of 'bogus' marriages among Asians was a few cases of wives writing letters to the Home Office, asking for their troublesome husbands to be removed. The woman could simply inform the Home Office that her husband thinks he has now got permanent stay in this country but that it is really just a marriage of convenience for him, entered into so he can remain in Britain. Other cases became known as those of 'reluctant brides' (see Shah 1979), where fiancées were seeking to prevent the entry of a man chosen for them. This in turn led to allegations of widespread 'forced marriages' (see Poulter 1986:22-33).

It appears that some women started informing the Home Office in this way, sometimes as a device to make the husband behave in a more agreeable way, a strategy that is quite common in the subcontinent but that badly backfired in several cases in Britain. If such a marriage was then, upon examination, deemed to be an attempt at evasion of the Rules, deportation as conducive to the public good was possible and indeed probable (see Mahmud Khan [1983] QB 79O; *Mohd. Malik* [1981] Imm AR 134; *Ullah* [1982] Imm AR 124; *Osama* [1978] Imm AR 8). These dragnet probationary provisions meant firstly that leave to remain automatically lapsed on breakdown of a marriage, even if it was initially a genuine one. Secondly, all husbands had to comply with this rule after entry to Britain, even if their marriage had taken place many years before entry.

It is very important to emphasise here that the new rules on probationary periods allowed the Home Office to ask all kinds of further questions about a couple's circumstances and to probe into personal and intimate details of individual marriages and of marriage arrangements among South Asians generally. The practical experience gained in this way was soon to be exploited.

The possibility of intrusive questioning by immigration officials as to the state and details of a particular marriage now became a new area of concern. While M.P.s had been assured that the 1977 Rules were designed to prevent 'bogus marriages', they were also told on 10th January 1978 that the new Rules would not affect the many genuine and lasting marriages which are arranged in accordance with Asian culture (see Bhabha et al. 1985:55). The issue had also been discussed in the House of Lords (*H.L. Debates* [10 May 1977], cols. 218-9) and an assurance was given by the Home Office Minister that intrusive questioning would not be allowed (*H.C. Debates* [24 May 1977], cols.1356-7). However, it is apparent that these assurances were later broken and that the Home Office began to 'discover' the further and immense potential for intensive questioning of the spouses, which gradually became a central technique of immigration control. Detailed material on this particular issue is provided by a J.C.W.I. study about checks on immigrant marriages (1977) and by Lal and Wilson (1986).

Yet, as we saw, the rule changes of 1977, directed as they were mainly at fiancés, were of course incapable of stopping male immigration from the subcontinent altogether and a significant number of South Asian men continued to come to Britain as spouses. This led to further attempts to reduce the numbers of male immigrants.

At this crucial time, a Conservative government was elected in April 1979 on a manifesto which pledged to tighten immigration controls and to refuse entry to any husbands and fiancés. The argumentation for this had been prepared by an all-party Select Committee on Race Relations and Immigration, which provided a first report in 1978 (HMSO: HC 303) and had focused very much on the issue of men joining women, which was seen as a violation of customary traditions and as evidence of purposeful circumvention of British immigration rules. Bhabha et al. (1985:56-57) report in considerable detail about the conclusions of the Committee, which 'were based on the assumption that wives were by definition dependent on their husbands' and that, as prospective heads of families, fiancés were entering the UK 'not so much to join a family as to form a new one' (see Bhabha et al. 1985:56).

Matters of race relations formed an important part of this debate and much lipservice was paid to the need to acknowledge and respect the cultural patterns of ethnic minorities in a multi-racial society. This argument was, however, turned around to remind Asians that they themselves should pay greater regard to the mores of their country of adoption and to their own traditional pattern of the bride joining the husband's family (Bhabha et al. 1985:56).

This particular issue, then, received a lot of attention in 1978-79. This points to official anxiety about being 'tricked' by Asians, while no real attempt is made to understand and to study the customary laws of South Asians and their implications in Britain's immigration context. It is relevant to point out here that even today the very same issues are still prominent, as Asian women in

Britain continue to marry men from South Asia and expect them to join their wives in Britain (see Powell 1990:107-108; Powell 1991, part 6).

Instead of seeking to understand the socio-legal implications of British immigration controls for the ethnic minority communities, politicians played with more sophisticated regulatory mechanisms. In a speech in April 1978, William Whitelaw, then the Home Affairs spokesman of the Conservative opposition, expressed the intention of a future Conservative government to introduce more restrictions on the right of entry of husbands and fiancés. He argued along familiar lines, claiming that there was widespread abuse of British immigration control through the practice of arranged marriages. He also sought to reinforce the 'reasonable' notion that it would be in accordance with European as well as Indian customs that the patrilocal residence pattern was the norm (for details see Bhabha et al. 1985:57).

Against this, Samir Shah (1979) put the rather different views of the Asian community, explaining above all that the patrilocal residence pattern was, in India, the traditional normal rule, but this had long been modified as a result of urbanisation and industrial development. Thus, many men moved to the place from where their wives or fiancés came. But — this is the important innovation, common to the Indian and British experience — they then stayed either with members of their own family, or the couple established its own new residence, so that we get what sociologists call a 'neolocal' pattern, and 'the wife does leave her parental home' (Shah 1979:132). There is also long-standing evidence of modification of traditional patrilocal customs, so that some men would move to the place of residence of their wife (see e.g. Powell 1991: Sheet 6.0). Though it might involve a loss of status for the man, it may be economically beneficial to both spouses and her family to have this arrangement, especially if the girl's parents are short of male manpower, for example. More importantly, as one can observe within the communities, custom allows for a matrilocal pattern when the daughter is an only child, or when the other siblings live far away from the parents.

Shah's article also contains an interesting discussion about the allegation that Asian dowry payments have changed in character as a result of immigration advantages, insinuating that Asian men could virtually buy their entry rights to Britain (see also Powell 1991: Sheet 5.1). Further, Shah (1979:132) provides a neat summary of the British perception of Asian arranged marriages as purposely designed to achieve immigration:

> 'Thus, all Asian men entering Britain for marriage may be presumed to be flouting the traditions of the genuine Asian arranged marriage. All such marriages become *a priori* suspect.'

Despite evidence that the number of husbands admitted was really quite insignificant for a country of more than 50 million people, with an increase from 277 in 1974 to 3005 in 1978 (Shah 1979:132), public concern about that increase led to definite plans by the Conservatives to curtail the entry rights of all husbands and fiancés. Once the Conservatives had been elected on their anti-immigration manifesto in April 1979, Britain's first female Prime Minister set about to introduce a new set of Immigration Rules that would again deprive all women of the right to be joined by their spouses.

It has been shown that this was opposed not only in Parliament by individuals like David Steel, who had earlier voiced much disquiet about the 1968 legislation (Steel 1969), but also by women's organisations and numerous black groups (for details see Bhabha et al.1985:57-59). Clearly, the planned total ban on the entry rights of husbands and fiancés ran into fierce opposition from all quarters but, again, most concern was voiced about the curtailment of the rights of white women. As Bhabha et al. (1985:58-59) demonstrate, failure to recognise the social, racial and cultural differences between British women prevented, at this point, a united front against the new Rules and led, yet gain, to a new regime of discriminatory regulation in British immigration control that hit non-white people.

A White Paper (Cmnd. 7750) in November 1979 set out the proposals for revision of the Immigration Rules to be laid before Parliament. Regarding husbands and fiancés, paragraph 10 of the proposals (p. iv) stated unambiguously that the new draft Rules,

'...are designed to curtail the exploitation of marriage as a means of primary immigration. In future husbands and fiancés will not be permitted to enter or remain if there is reason to believe that settlement in this country is the main motive of the marriage. Moreover, the wife must be a citizen of of the United Kingdom and Colonies born in this country.'

Clearly, as a result of widespread protests, the original plan of refusing entry to the husbands and fiancés of all women settled in Britain had been abandoned by the Home Secretary. Instead, an arbitrary distinction had been drawn between women who were born in Britain and those who were not. It was now proposed that the latter were to be banned from bringing in their husbands and fiancés.

This proposal, designed to give greater protection to white British women than the original plan, in fact exempted most of them from the new form of discrimination, which was clearly aimed at reducing non-white male immigration to Britain (Bhabha et al. 1985:59). Comparatively little was made of the racial distinction, though, as the protests against the proposals in the White Paper focused on the fact that many white British women would still be hit by the new Rules, for example if their parents had worked abroad when they were born. Press coverage and even official intervention (for details see Bhabha et al. 1985:59) whipped up so much opposition that the Government, by December 1979, had to work on a revision of the proposals.

When the new Rules were drawn up in their final form in February 1980, they took particular account of the position of white British women and discriminated quite clearly against most non-white women settled in Britain. The new Rules (HC 394), to which we shall turn in detail below, allowed only female citizens of the United Kingdom and Commonwealth born in Britain, and also those with at least one parent born in Britain, to bring in their husbands and fiancés from abroad. This is a kind of patriality clause designed to exclude those female Citizens of the United Kingdom and Colonies (CUKCs) who had earlier acquired citizenship through registration or naturalisation, as many women of South Asian origin would have done. This, then, was a clear case of discrimination against women of non-British ancestry, modelled perhaps on the regulations of the *Commonwealth Immigrants Act* of 1968, which made similar distinctions. The new Rules thus enforced, as Bhabha et al. (1985:60) rightly emphasise, a two-tier citizenship, a device and concept that would soon be still more elaborately used in the *British Nationality Act* of 1981.

■ 3.5.2 The Immigration Rules of 1980 (HC 394)

The proposed changes found favour with a larger Parliamentary majority than the previous proposals; HC 394, the new set of British Immigration Rules, came into force on 1st March 1980.

The effect of these Rules, as a result of explicit discrimination against certain groups of British women, was first of all to abandon the principle that all women whose permanent home was in the UK should be able to live here with their husbands. This, compared to the law in other European countries, and to the position of EEC citizen women resident in the UK, was clearly a significant deprivation of an important legal right. In the European context, it laid the new Rules open to serious challenge, a matter to which we return later.

Pressure was now again exercised on many non-white women to join a spouse overseas, rather than attempting to bring the male spouse to the UK. A major implication of the new Rules, as we shall see, was a hidden repatriation strategy, which is clearly exemplified by the wording of paragraph 54 of HC 394 (see below, p.68) which makes quite specific provisions for fiancés wishing to come to Britain to get married to a British-based woman, who would then leave Britain with the 'passenger' within three months.

Significantly, an equivalent provision is no longer found in the current set of Immigration Rules (HC 251). It must have soon become clear that this kind of benign provision could not be very useful in practice. Firstly, marrying in Britain is probably much more costly than in India, where one has the added advantage of being able to invite the whole extended family and anyone else who matters. Secondly, nobody seems to have considered the immigration implications of paragraph 54 in terms of visitors. If a complete extended clan of the fiancé's side wished to attend a wedding in Britain, it would not only be costly in air fares, but we can be sure that entry clearance officers would get terribly concerned and would declare themselves not satisfied that all these people would in fact return to the subcontinent, especially if they were young male family members. The fact that we never heard of whole wedding parties arriving in Heathrow from South Asia clearly shows that the scheme of paragraph 54 was quite impracticable, but clearly sinister; it was not a realistic possibility for many fiancés to come to Britain for marriage only. Our conclusion on this point clearly implies that the repatriation strategy of this interesting paragraph would not work in practice.

The stipulation that the British-based woman or one of her parents must have been born in the UK was quite obviously discriminatory against those women who were, for example, merely settled in the UK. Such women now had no right to be joined by their husband or fiancé, and they could not acquire that right either, even if they became a UK citizen.

The public debate at the time focused on the rights of women to sponsor a husband or fiancé; this is also clearly reflected in the comments made by those who wrote about this period. The new Immigration Rules, however, hardly ever mentioned wives and contained quite specific rules for husbands and fiancés, including, for the first time ever, an explicit mention of the concept of 'primary purpose'. The relevant paras of the 1980 Rules (H.C. 394) are set out below. They are paras 50-51 dealing with husbands, paras 52-54 concerning fiancés, and para 55 dealing with fiancées.

Paragraph 50 of HC 394 reads:

'50. The husband of a woman who is settled in the U.K., or who is on the same occasion being admitted for settlement, is to be admitted if he holds a current entry clearance granted to him for that purpose. An entry clearance will be refused if the E.C.O. has reason to believe:

(a) that the marriage was one entered into primarily to obtain admission to the United Kingdom; or

(b) that one of the parties no longer has any intention of living permanently with the other as his or her spouse; or

(c) that the parties to the marriage have not met.

A marriage to which none of (a) to (c) above applies gives a man no claim to enter but an entry clearance may be issued provided that the wife is a citizen of the United Kingdom and Colonies born in the United Kingdom.

51. A passenger who holds an entry clearance issued under the preceding paragraph should, subject to paragraph 13, be admitted for an initial period of up to 12 months provided that leave to enter shall not be refused on grounds of restricted returnability or on medical grounds.'

Paragraphs 52-54 of the same Rules, relating to fiancés, state:

'52. A man seeking to enter the United Kingdom for marriage to a woman settled here and who intends himself to settle thereafter should not be admitted unless he holds a current entry clearance granted to him for that purpose. An entry clearance will be refused if the entry clearance officer has reason to believe:

(a) that the primary pupose of the intended marriage is to obtain admission to the United Kingdom; or

(b) that there is no intention that the parties to the marriage should live together permanently as man and wife; or

(c)   that the parties to the proposed marriage have not met.

Where none of (a) to (c) above applies a man has no claim to admission for the purpose of marriage but an entry clearance may be issued provided that the woman is a citizen of the United Kingdom and Colonies born in the United Kingdom. An entry clearance should not be issued unless the entry clearance officer is satisfied that adequate maintenance and accommodation will be available for the fiancé until the date of his marriage without the need to have recourse to public funds.

53. A man holding an entry clearance issued under the preceding paragraph should, subject to paragraph 13, be admitted for 3 months and advised to apply to the Home Office once the marriage has taken place for an extension of stay. A prohibition on employment should be imposed.

54. A man seeking limited leave to enter the United Kingdom for marriage to a woman settled here may be admitted only if the Immigration Officer is satisfied that the marriage will take place within a reasonable time; that the passenger and his wife will leave the United Kingdom shortly after the marriage; and that the requirements of paragraph 17 are met. Where the Immigration Officer is so satisfied, the passenger may be admitted for 3 months, with a prohibition on employment.'

While these Rules do not say anything specifically about wives, there is a single paragraph about fiancées, which reads as follows:

'55. A woman seeking to enter to marry a man settled in the United Kingdom should be admitted if the Immigration Officer is satisfied that the marriage will take place within a reasonable time and that adequate maintenance and accommodation will be available, without the need to have recourse to public funds, both before and after the marriage. She may be admitted for a period of up to 3 months subject to a condition prohibiting the taking of employment and should be advised to apply to the Home Office for an extension of stay once the marriage has taken place.'

We shall analyse the application of the primary purpose rule under HC 394 in detail in the following sub-chapter. Here, it is important to point out that the new Rules had an instant and considerable impact on the numbers of South Asian males gaining entry to Britain. Thus, in terms of immigration control itself, the new regime appears to have been very successful. While the total number for fiancés entering from all countries but India fell by over 1,000 between 1977 and 1980, the number for India alone fell by 1,400 in the same period (Bevan 1986:247-248; Evans 1983:133).

In the Indian subcontinent itself, the rule changes apparently had a dramatic effect. Applications by husbands and fiancés fell from 3,660 in 1979 to 820 in 1980 (Bevan 1986:248). For a simplistic observer, at long last here was a successful means of immigration control, hitting the desired target group very effectively. For those who fixed their eyes on immigration statistics, this was good news. Of course, the new Rules quite clearly and inevitably discriminated against the recently arrived and predominantly 'coloured' immigrants and were striking at the custom of arranged marriages (Bevan 1986:248), but surely, concerns of 'national interest' and 'public policy' should be allowed to override the traditions of ethnic minorities? We shall see further below that this Anglo-centric approach was not maintainable for long.

☐ 3.5.3 The application of the primary purpose rule

It is important to emphasise at the outset of this sub-chapter that although the term 'primary purpose' was used explicitly for the first time in the 1980 set of Immigration Rules (HC 394), it did not immediately attract much attention, nor did it become as central in practice as from 1982/3 onwards (Macdonald 1987:233; Macdonald and Blake 1991:260).

None of the existing studies on British immigration law has covered the gradual development of the primary purpose rule in full depth. The most comprehensive piece on the topic so far was written by Marrington (1985). An attempt is made here to bring together the widely dispersed material on the topic and to analyse the process of development of the primary purpose rule by a detailed study of changes in the Immigration Rules. The result has been a rather large chapter, necessarily divided into several sub-sections: the first deals with the period immediately after 1980, in which the p.p.r. is still a minor issue and develops, as it were, 'under cover'. The second part focuses on the new requirement that the parties must have met, with its related attack on Asian arranged marriages, while the third sub-section considers the effects of pressure from the European Commission of Human Rights, which had a not entirely beneficial effect on the development of Britain's Immigration Rules. The fourth part briefly lays out the relevant provisions of the rule changes brought in by HC 169 in 1983, while the fifth section covers in more detail the full-blown development of the p.p.r. after 1983. Subsequent parts focus on more recent changes to the Immigration Rules in 1985 (HC 503) and 1990 (HC 251), laying out their respective requirements with particular reference to the primary purpose rule and related issues.

☐ 3.5.3.1 The undercover development of the p.p.r.

As we saw above, sex discrimination was inherent in the scheme of the Immigration Rules of 1980 (HC 394) with its 'extraordinary provisions' (Evans 1983:134). A woman settled in Britain was now not necessarily able to sponsor her partner, unlike every settled man. Clearly, this approach is based on the assumption that women should be dependent on men, rather than vice versa, and it represented a step back from the enlightened non-discriminatory approach taken in 1974.

Despite the opposition to South Asian immigration generally and evidence that more than twice as many South Asian women than men came to Britain for settlement between 1973 and 1983 (see detailed statistics at Bhabha et al. 1985:62), it was apparently felt that South Asian men should retain the right to bring in a spouse, because traditionally it had been the practice in Asian cultures for women to follow men on marriage and to settle in the husband's place of residence. Also, by 1980 there were still a substantial number of South Asian men who had come to Britain much earlier and who had not, for various reasons, called over their spouse or family. Their rights to family reunion had been expressly preserved in section 1(5) of the *Immigration Act* of 1971 and were not touched at this time. In this context, there is evidence that the various Asian communities in Britain followed a different pattern of family reunification. Muslim men, in particular Bangladeshis, often delayed this process of family reunion (Sondhi 1987:19). Later, as is well-known, they became the major victims of new rules on the entry of wives and children.

The focus of the 1980 set of Immigration Rules was, as we already saw, on the position and motivations of those men who had married or were proposing to marry British women that could sponsor a man to join them in accordance with HC 394. It appears that the existing literature has not looked at this group of men in any detail. We must assume, first of all, that there were not many men in this particular category. Secondly, those who fell into it would surely be examined and assessed by different criteria, depending on their own ethnic background and that of their sponsor. Thus, we hear nothing more, it appears, of any cases involving white British women seeking to be joined by a man from overseas whose case is rejected. It is possible and indeed likely, however, that the applications of non-white men seeking to join white British women were scrutinised in more detail. But, aware of the impending challenge to the 1980 Immigration Rules from the European Court of Human Rights, the British immigration authorities must have been concerned not to create fresh test cases, so that most of these men were rather likely to be given entry clearance and, later, permanent settlement rights.

Considerable hardship was, however, experienced by non-white British women who sought to be joined by a spouse or fiancé. In the majority of cases, their husband or fiancé would himself be non-white, and we can be sure that his motivations would now be scrutinised in much more detail. As we saw above (p.76), notice to this effect had already been given in Cmnd 7750 of November 1979. At this time, though, the subsequent Rules in HC 394 still place the burden of proof on the immigration authorities, so that a man seeking to marry a British-based woman, or a husband of such a woman, could not be rejected if the conditions laid down in paras 50 or 52 of HC 394 had been satisfied.

However, let us remind ourselves that entry clearance could be refused to a husband,

> '... if the entry clearance officer has reason to believe... that the marriage was one entered into primarily to obtain admission to the United Kingdom..' (HC 394, para 50).

Thus, as Evans (1983:134) points out, the power to refuse entry clearance or leave to remain indefinitely after 12 months on the basis of 'primary purpose' is already there at this point. The above rule allowed officers to question the motives of male applicants to join their wife and to form their own opinion about what they heard and saw. Similarly, the fiancé rules in para 52 make the granting of entry clearance dependent on the officer's discretion in assessing the available evidence. It is apparent that this discretion can be used flexibly and can be employed to reject a large number of applicants.

It appears, though, that this did not in fact happen straight away, though there was considerable disquiet about intrusive questioning. Bhabha et al. (1985:61) indicate that the new clause 'was used relatively sparingly at first', but 'it has increasingly operated to keep out Asian husbands and fiancés'. There is an apparently simple explanation for this slow process of developing the primary purpose rule. As Ian Macdonald (1987:233) has shown:

> 'Until HC 169 came into force it was simpler to refuse husbands' and male fiancés' applications on the basis that their wife or fiancée, although a British citizen, was not born in the UK. This effectively excluded the husbands of all but a few women who were settled in the UK and in particular it effectively prevented the arrival of husbands and fiancés from the Indian subcontinent, who were the main target of the husband rule.'

In other words, by attaching the prohibition on entry to the legal position of the female sponsor, there was no need to develop the concept of 'primary purpose'. But while this is correct for the vast majority of cases, the few husbands and fiancés who could still apply under paras 50 and 52 of HC 394 would offer an opportunity to entry clearance officers to rehearse their processing of such applications and to develop a taste for their increased discretionary powers. Nothing much has been made of this in the literature, it appears, but Ian Macdonald has ominously and rather cryptically stated that by the time the British government had to relax the requirements regarding the female sponsors in 1982/83,

> '... the primary purpose rule had become the principal instrument for controlling male immigration through marriage, particularly from the Indian subcontinent.' (Macdonald 1987:233).

There can be no doubt that this statement is factually correct, but how did this process develop? How did the primary purpose rule become the principal element of immigration control?

We have been unable to find much evidence of how this happened in particular cases soon after the 1980 rule changes. In principle, Macdonald is correct to emphasise that once the British government had dropped the requirement that a sponsoring wife or fiancée had to be born in the UK, and then that she had to be a UK citizen, the primary purpose rule remained, in fact, almost the only effective weapon left in its armoury. One must perhaps assume that the government, acting as it were against the wishes of some of its own MPs, only relaxed the official Immigration Rules once the surprisingly effective discretionary powers of immigration officials under those Rules had been tested sufficiently well and had been supplemented, as we shall see, with a crucial change, namely the shift of the burden of proof to the applicant.

But what happened in cases before the rule changes of 1982/3 where the primary purpose of the marriage could become an issue? Although he, too, focuses on the later period, Christopher Newdick (1985:816) points to the important change of emphasis in the application of the immigration officials' discretion to reject male applicants after 1980. He quotes Mr. Waddington, who in the Subcommitte on Race Relations in 1984 (HC 224, para 4) said, in essence, that men would now see their applications refused,

> 'where the marriage was a genuine one and the man perhaps was perfectly content to live with the woman for the rest of his natural life, but still his primary purpose in entering into that contract was to get to this country.'

In other words, immigration officials could now reject the applications of men who they knew were parties to genuine marriages that were intended to last lifelong. They could do this simply by claiming that they had reason to believe, in the case of husbands, 'that the marriage was one entered into primarily to obtain admission to the United Kingdom' (para 50[a] of HC 394). In the case of fiancés, it was similarly easy for officers to state that there was reason to believe 'that the primary purpose of the intended marriage is to obtain admission to the United Kingdom' (para 52 [a] of HC 394).

This new position at once raises the issue of relationship and relative importance of the respective three requirements in paras 50 and 52 of HC 394. If (b) and (c) were satisfied, could an application be rejected on the basis of (a) alone? This point was soon to be decided in a series of early cases on the primary purpose rule (see below, p.120ff.). At this time, the inherent discretion of the immigration officials allowed them to bring in their own, personal views of the subject. It is not surprising that in many later cases, quite apparently, this group of predominently white middle-aged male officers paid little attention to the human rights dimension and simply found themselves unable to have no reason to believe that male applicants from South Asia had primarily made their marriage arrangements with a view to settlement in Britain. This, of course, raises the difficult question of deciding which among the variety of purposes of a particular marriage is in fact the primary one (Newdick 1985:816).

While one cannot but agree with Newdick (1985:816) that it is in principle quite legitimate to exclude those who use marriage as a device for avoiding immigration controls, the same author points out the potential for abuse:

'On the other hand, if the rule is to be used against those whose marriages are acknowledged to be perfectly genuine, care must be taken to avoid using the rule in a way that is harsh and unfair and likely to offend a sense of justice.' (Newdick 1985:816).

As we emphasised before, quite unnoticed by a wider public, the immigration authorities began to test and use their discretionary powers against male applicants from South Asia. This may well be seen as the result of personal bias on the part of immigration officials, but there is some evidence that secret instructions to officials played their own role in this context, principally by admonishing officers — as if most of them needed this advice — that discretion should not necessarily be exercised in favour of the applicant. The fact that such instructions came to light much later indicates that the Home Office and its personnel did not merely stumble across a new difficult problem, but that there was in fact an undercover operation to experiment with the effectiveness of the primary purpose rule, as introduced into HC 394.

Thus, at an early stage in the application of HC 394, in the few cases that fell to be decided, the intricate exclusionary mechanisms of the primary purpose rule were being developed and tested *in camera*. There would initially have been a trend to accept many marriages as perfectly genuine and to come to a finding, looking at the evidence 'as a whole' (Mole 1987:29), therefore, that it could not be the primary purpose of the man to come to Britain. The result, the granting of an entry clearance or of permanent settlement rights, may be seen as a victory of common sense, but every case so decided contributed to the statistics which showed that men continued to come to Britain to join their female partners. Since these statistics were eagerly watched, any evidence of increase would immediately inspire new efforts to tighten the control system further. All one needed was immigration officials who gradually developed a perception of desperate South Asian males who were queueing up all over the world to come to Britain by marrying the right kind of woman. They could then reject any male applicant, as they wished. This developing trend was certainly supported by Home Office instructions that were not made public, but reinforced the xenophobic perceptions of those people that mattered most, namely the immigration officials who made the front-line decisions.

At the same time, we must remember, the 1980 Rules faced the looming threat of an adverse decision from Strasbourg. There was also much public opposition to the newly instituted discriminatory regime of British immigration control in Britain itself.

In this situation, reform proposals would be aimed at restoring the rights of all women to bring in a spouse of their choice, thus reducing the obvious racial discrimination in the new Rules. However, if one were to follow this route, the immigration statistics would very soon set the alarm bells ringing again, sparking off new moves to curtail the entry of family members from certain countries.

In this new episode of conflict between equal rights and immigration phobia, there followed a vigorous public debate about the potential for reforms. At the same time, rather less publicly, immigration officials continued to apply their mind to the issue of primary purpose. It comes as no surprise that the ease with which the officials' discretion under the Rules could be increased without any changes in the law must have struck ministers as the most promising way forward. Thus it became possible to give in, to some extent, to the public demands for legal reform, while one could maintain, at the same time, a catchy discourse of double-speak, emphasising that immigration controls were essential for good race relations, while non-white persons found themselves increasingly powerless against official discretion exercised by a legal system that could claim to be non-discriminatory.

☐ 3.5.3.2 The requirement to have met: Attacking arranged marriages

Before we turn to the rule changes in 1982/83 to see how the government finally introduced the p.p.r. more explicitly, we need to consider briefly another aspect of the husband and fiancé rules which has given rise to many comments, though it has not been a very important issue in legal practice. The reasons for this will be explained below. The requirement to have met is relevant here since the development of the p.p.r. cannot be fully understood as a technical legal mechanism; it must also be seen in the context of a cultural struggle between British core values (on this see Poulter 1986:vi and Poulter 1987) and the quite different value systems of the various immigrant communities. Certainly, when it comes to arranged marriages, there are widely divergent and conflicting views, depending on the observer's viewpoint (see in detail Poulter 1986:22-33; Bradley 1983; Ballard 1978; Pearl 1987). Interestingly, English courts have added their voice to this debate (see *Hirani* v. *Hirani* [1983] 4 FLR 232 [CA]), which is by no means conclusive, as a recent suggestion that *Hirani* was decided *per incuriam* confirms (see J. C. Hall in Vol. 51, part 2 [July 1992] *The Cambridge Law Journal*, p. 387).

Virtually all writers agree that the imposition of the new requirement in paras 50(c) and 52(c) of HC 394 that the parties to a marriage or proposed marriage should have met was specifically aimed at the South Asian custom of arranged marriages (see e.g., Sondhi 1987:15; Bhabha et al. 1985:60-64; Evans 1983:134-135). At the same time it specifically hit poorer people (Bhabha et al. 1985: 60-61) and those women who were already being discriminated against by the Immigration Rules of 1980 in that these Rules allowed only patrial women to sponsor a spouse. Thus, the new law discriminated indirectly against non-white women, as it was,

> '..likely to affect only women whose parents had emigrated from the Indian sub-continent, and who wished to maintain the custom of the arranged marriage by selecting for their daughters prospective husbands from their country of origin.' (Evans 1983:134-135).

The additional requirement that the spouses should have met never became as important in its own right as the matter of primary purpose, or now the maintenance and accommodation requirements (Gillespie 1992). The requirement that the parties should have met is still present in the current set of Immigration Rules (HC 251, paras 47[c] and 50[c]), but the interpretations of this rule do not appear to be very strict (see Macdonald and Blake 1991:266) and have not even received much attention till recently (Macdonald 1987:237). It would therefore appear that this particular rule has rather more cultural than legal implications. It has certainly given rise to some interesting debates about the place of ethnic minority cultures in Britain, about race relations, and the difficult issue of assimilation, all of which are too wide for our present ambit.

Was it really necessary to introduce an added condition that the spouses must have met, or do we need to assume simply official hardheadedness or a form of cultural imperialism? Marrington (1985:539) provides evidence of an official statement to the effect that marriages of convenience had been adequately dealt with already by the 1977 Rules. However, this means probably that the detection of actual sham marriages had been facilitated by the 1977 Rules, whereas here we find, of course, a new form of alleged 'marriage of convenience' which we have already seen earlier. It is that type of marriage in which South Asian husbands or fiancés seek to join their female partners in Britain, rather than expecting the women to settle in the subcontinent. In other words, we are back to the suspicion of 'bogus immigration marriages' that has been cast on virtually all Asian arranged marriages.

Obviously, linked to the issue of 'marriage of convenience', the requirement could imply an official expectation that individuals who have actually met are more likely to be parties to genuine marriages. But this is not conclusive in itself, as the parties may in fact have met for the purpose of arranging a sham marriage. If that was the primary purpose of the marriage, it would probably be normal that the 'spouses' had negotiated the arrangement, unless this was done entirely through third parties, which is of course possible.

The requirement that the spouses should have met could simply be seen as an indicator of the genuineness of a particular marriage. But this is indeed too simple. It continues to be common practice among South Asians, also in Britain, that there is minimal contact between spouses till they are actually fully married. Menski (1987: 194-195) has shown how in Britain the official registration of a Hindu marriage is often seen as the formal equivalent of an engagement rather than the conclusion of a marriage that has full legal validity, with the effect that the spouses may remain virtual strangers to each other till the customary wedding rituals have been concluded. Marriage is here seen as a complex process of becoming husband and wife, rather than a simple contractual arrangement, and there can be no doubt that the immigration authorities' approach to South Asian marriages is culturally and ideologically biased, leading to hard cases that may leave a bitter taste of injustice.

As already indicated earlier, it is quite likely that the official approach to Asian arranged marriages in the immigration context was informed by a perception that many arranged marriages are in fact forced marriages (see Poulter 1986:22-33). This would, in the immigration context, lead to the allegation that South Asian women growing up in Britain were forced by their families to marry a man from the subcontinent, just so that he could come to the UK. However (see p.57), this does not appear to be a realistic assessment of the actual social situation 'on the ground'. It seems a much more important consideration that young South Asian women growing up in Britain should find appropriate spouses, which means, in most cases, a marriage partner from one's own community. It will be apparent that in most Asian communities the range and choice of potential marriage partners is much larger in the subcontinent than in Britain, thus requiring the arrangement of international marriages. However, to get to know a spouse who is thousands of miles away would certainly mean a lot of extra expense. Expecting this investment to be made, the 1980 Rules about having met appear designed to reduce Asian immigration rather than to prevent 'bogus marriages' (Bhabha et al. 1985:61).

There may be some effect of the rule that spouses should have met, however, in that it has now become much more common practice, in view of questions asked by ECOs and other officials at a later stage, that potential spouses meet and discuss their common future, at least to some extent. This strategy, again, brings with it new dangers which will be explained further below when we come to the case-law. In essence, what if a British Asian woman makes it a condition of the marriage that her spouse will settle with her in the UK? Here, again, there is a no-win situation if the immigration authorities argue that it must, then, be the primary purpose of any man who marries such a woman to come to the UK.

Breach of the requirement that the parties have met need not imply illegal entry. Indeed, it seemed to Lord Scarman (quoted by Bevan 1986:248) to be,

> 'An attack on the social habits and custom of people who have come to this country and who are living according to the customs in which they were brought up.'

When one considers this issue in the context of race relations, it is hardly a step forward that the government should seek to interfere in the marriage customs of South Asians, which are of such central relevance to people of any culture. When the government was pressed on this point, it was, as we saw, continuously unable to provide precise evidence of the level of abuse of arranged marriages. Bevan (1986:248) states:

'Admittedly it is impossible to reach a precise figure but one would normally expect some statistical evidence in similarly controversial areas. The truth may be that, in a field of general political consensus, justification can be sought in shared generalities and fears rather than figures.'

It would appear that the surreptitious development of the primary purpose rule under HC 394, shown in the previous sub-chapter, has been supported by the enquiry into whether the spouses have actually been able or willing to build up a close relationship. Lack of evidence on this could now not only lead to a finding that the parties to the marriage or intended marriage had not met, but could lead to a refusal of the application on the ground of primary purpose itself. All one needed was immigration officials who felt that a marriage or proposed marriage in which the spouses had not developed a personal relationship was really a marriage designed to achieve immigration advantages and was therefore automatically hit by the primary purpose rule. Conversely, there is anecdotal evidence to the effect that a couple's claim to have had a love match will facilitate the entry of the male spouse.

Since, as we saw already, the obsession with the idea that all South Asian male applicants were desperate to enter Britain as spouses became so strong, it became simple, in many cases, to come to a finding that the spouses had not met and to reject applications on this ground. But in practice, there is little evidence that this happened at once after the rule changes of 1980. Again, the explanation for this is probably easy. First of all, we may return to Ian Macdonald's argument that after 1979 it was initially not necessary to reject applications on any other ground than that the woman was not entitled to sponsor a spouse (see above, p.71). Then, once the Rules were changed in 1982 and 1983, so that more husbands had in fact *locus standi* to file an application, recourse to the immigration officer's reason to believe that the primary purpose of the marriage was settlement in the UK was sufficient to reject applicants. In fact, it was probably much easier to take that route with its subjective assessment than to develop the argument that a particular couple had not met, which would require a much more objective and factual approach. Indeed, even when the couple had met, and when all other conditions had been fulfilled, immigration officials could still reject the man's application on the ground of primary purpose.

This shows that, in legal practice, the requirement that the spouses should have met was really quite soon overshadowed and almost made redundant by the primary purpose rule itself. This view seems to be supported by the current textbooks which, as we saw, do not give much importance to the requirement that the spouses must have met.

There is an additional interesting aspect of the requirement to have met. As indicated, this rule may also have been designed to curtail the stricter forms of marriage arrangement in which the spouses are not allowed to meet before the actual marriage takes place. It has been claimed that the new legal requirements were probably designed to destroy this tradition, though this has been officially denied (Bhabha et al. 1985:60). In practice, this immigration requirement may have led to social change, in that now more families would allow young couples to communicate with each other before marriage, maybe under supervision, from a safe distance, or at least by phone. Such evidence could be useful in practice, especially since entry clearance officers and other officials may ask a wide range of searching questions about details of the couple's relationship. As we shall see later, the issue of 'intervening devotion' has become an important factor.

Such forms of social change may be seen as useful, since forced marriages are clearly not an acceptable way of arranging marriages among young people of any culture today. If the Immigration Rules hit poorer applicants more, they also had disproportionately negative effects on ultra-traditional marriage arrangements. The relatively higher refusal rates for Muslim men may, in part, be explained by this factor. It is too simple, though, to welcome such constraints unreservedly. They are, as Bhabha et al. (1985:61) emphasise, in the first place a cynical denial of the basic human rights of South Asian women by English law.

The requirements of HC 394 appear to make no substantial distinction between husbands and fiancés and would, therefore, probably hit fiancés much more effectively than husbands. This would lead, in turn, to a preference for marrying in South Asia rather than in Britain, making it more difficult to argue that the spouses have not met. Though it will be virtually impossible to prove this statistically, the growing preference after 1980 for applications as a spouse rather than as a fiancé must have made the requirement to have met more and more redundant. Here, too, we see, on the other side, the usefulness of the primary purpose rule which could be invoked despite the existence of a perfectly good and valid marriage.

Conversely, a later consequence of the refusals of husbands under the primary purpose rule has been that more Asian families have become reluctant about committing themselves to full marriages, so that fiancé and fiancée cases are still prominent today. Clearly, if one faces a very high probability that the man's application may attract a refusal, it is safer for the woman, and better for the status of the family, if the couple remain engaged rather than fully married. This in turn, as we shall see, has not only led to new legal arguments, but also to a much more cautious approach of British Asian families towards the arrangement of matches in South Asia. This deterrent effect of the primary purpose refusals is, of course, rather beneficial for British immigration control policies and may be seen as an effective way to weaken the tendency to make Asian international marriage arrangements.

An interesting question arose in cases of spouses who were married, but had not actually met, i.e. in the rare cases of proxy marriages. The 1980 Rules certainly constitute an implied attack on the potential for such marriages. They are not frequent, but may occur among South Asians in certain situations; they have certainly been seen as a potentially devious device to arrange immigration marriages. Pearl (1986:55-56) has argued that British practice is to recognise proxy marriages among Muslims, while he puts forward the view that:

'Proxy marriages using photographs or swords are not valid forms of marriage for the Hindu and Sikh communities.' (Pearl 1986:56).

This approach relies on an earlier article (Bradford 1975). However, the opinions expressed there are clearly misguided and are based on an incorrect interpretation of the requirements of Hindu law in India. In essence, Bradford's claim is:

'It is generally accepted that the two customs common to all Hindus are the invocation before the sacred fire, and the Saptapadi, the seven steps taken jointly by bride and groom. This seems to rule out the validity of a marriage in the absence of either partner.'(Bradford 1975:254).

It has been shown more recently that the custom of taking the seven steps is not at all a uniform legal requirement in Hindu law (Menski 1987:184-188); Indian case-law could be cited to support that position more firmly. To claim that marriages by proxy are not legally valid among Hindus is, therefore, an incorrect interpretation of the position in Indian law and, on no account, represents 'impeccable law', as the author somewhat arrogantly claimed (Bradford 1975:255). It would go too far here to argue in detail why proxy marriages among persons governed by South Asian Hindu laws should be accepted as legally valid; there is certainly a need to look at this issue afresh. A perceptive legal adviser would at least have pointed to the well-established presumption of marriage among Hindus (see Desai 1982:748).

Bradford's case concerned a couple that had been married for many years, while immigration officials will often deal with spouses that have recently been married or are still engaged only. Bradford himself indicated that the case he referred to caused considerable indignation and a profound feeling of injustice. Similarly, to find one's application for entry clearance rejected on the basis of a finding that the spouses have not met, will often lead to a feeling of being discriminated against by English law. This could clearly not be conducive to good race relations, so it appears that the low-key approach to the requirement that the spouses must have met is at the same time evidence of a combination of multiple political expediencies and of the much superior force and potential of the primary purpose rule, to which we now need to turn in more detail again.

☐ 3.5.3.3 The pressure from Europe

We have seen that the openly discriminatory Immigration Rules contained in HC 394 of 1980 sparked off concerted criticism as soon as they had come into operation. Marrington (1985:539) has emphasised:

'It was soon apparent that the overt sex discrimination within the provisions would be indefensible in the wider international community.'

Criticising the 'complicated but cunning provisions of the 1980 Rules', Bhabha et al. (1985:64) provide considerable detail about the emerging protest movement in Britain against inhuman immigration controls generally as well as the more specific campaigns directed at alleviating the suffering of individual applicants who got entangled in the new provisions.

Bhabha et al. (1985:64-65) felt, though, that even the combined strength of feminist, anti-racist and pro-immigrant movements and campaigns in Britain was not able, by itself, to bring about meaningful changes. The government, having seized the moral high ground over immigration by using public policy arguments, could simply more or less ignore these non-establishment protests, however embarrassing they were. On the other hand, pressure from the European Commission of Human Rights proved to be the crucial factor in the process of changing the 1980 Immigration Rules. As we shall see below, this did not have a totally positive effect, as the 1983 Rules contain, in fact, an even more discriminatory set of provisions than the earlier Rules. Significantly in 1992, after the test case of *Surinder Singh*, we find a similar constellation and familiar apprehensions. One may therefore predict, with some certainty, that the exclusionary mechanisms of the primary purpose rule today will be maintained and may in fact be strengthened through yet more sophisticated rule changes.

The 1980 Rules constituted a clear case of sexual discrimination, were obviously racially motivated, and appeared to amount to a violation of the right to family life in breach of the European Convention on Human Rights. However, pleas to articles 3 (inhuman treatment), 8 (family life), 13 (effective remedy before a national authority) and 14 (non-discrimination) of the Convention appeared to be insufficient at first, since the European Commission had earlier not objected to the argument that a woman could still join her husband abroad (*Papayianni* [1974] Imm AR 7; see Bevan 1986:248).

However, many women who were separated from their husbands by the 1980 Rules took their cases to the European Commission of Human Rights, which decided already in December 1980 that a hearing should be held to determine whether such cases could be referred to the European Court of Human Rights in Strasbourg. This hearing did not take place for another 17 months, though, indicating the intense lobbying behind the scenes, before finally in May 1982 the Commission declared the complaints admissible (for details see Evans 1983:135). Formal proceedings in three selected test cases were then prepared before the European Court of Human Rights in Strasbourg.

After the adverse comments about Britain's treatment of the Ugandan Asians (see *East African Asians* v. *United Kingdom* at [1981] 3 EHRR 76), the UK now found itself again under intense pressure to conform to international human rights standards and, in particular, to bring its domestic law on the settlement of spouses in line with European human rights law. A Home Affairs Committee of the House of Commons heard expert evidence about this matter, warning the UK government of impending defeat in these test cases (Evans 1983:135; Bevan 1986:248-249). In fact, the European Commission gave an opinion on 12th May 1983 (see Berger 1989:293) and found against the UK in October 1983 (Bevan 1986:249), while the Strasbourg Court finally ruled against the UK in its judgment of 28th May 1985 in *Abdulaziz, Cabales and Balkandali* ([1985] 7 EHRR 471; for details see Berger 1989:292-296 and chapter 3.5.3.6 below).

Under threat of the impending defeat from Strasbourg, desperate efforts were made in London to preserve the British system of law-making and to salvage as much as possible from the exclusionary mechanisms of the 1980 Immigration Rules. Some formal changes had to be made anyway because of the impending implementation of the *British Nationality Act*, 1981, so it was convenient to experiment with a few more amendments.

'In 1982, the Government, though refusing to admit it publicly, was sufficiently concerned about the progress of the cases before the Commission and about unease within its own backbenches, that it took the opportunity of amending the proviso as part of a package of changes.' (Bevan 1986:249).

The plan was, first of all, to allow entry or settlement to the husbands and fiancés of all women who were British citizens, regardless of how they had acquired that status. This was justified, as Evans (1983:136) shows very well, by quite disingenuous references to planned rule changes in British citizenship law, while the Government was rather silent about the impending threat of an unfavourable decision from Strasbourg. Clearly, the new rules would have led to the abolition of the rather racially motivated preferential treatment for patrial British women in the 1980 Rules.

However, it was immediately obvious that this rule change would lead to an estimated annual increase of about 2000-3000 applications by husbands or fiancés. Evans (1983:139) saw such figures as guesses, but any kind of increase, quite obviously, was not found acceptable by many Conservatives (for examples see Bevan 1986:249; Bhabha et al. 1985:66-67). Thus, a revised set of Immigration Rules was prepared and published in a White Paper (Cmnd 8683) in October 1982, to be introduced as HC 66 in Parliament in December 1982, and to have effect from 1st January 1983, the date on which the new British nationality law would become operative. However, this slick timetable was not quite maintainable, since the new proposals upset more or less everyone.

The new proposals were debated at length (*H.C. Debates* [11 November 1982], col. 692 and *H.L. Debates* [18 November 1982], col.671). The most significant of the proposals in the White Paper was the liberalisation of the rules regarding women's rights to sponsor a husband or fiancé. The proposed rule allowed applications for entry clearance or settlement for husbands and fiancés of any woman who was a British citizen, regardless of how she had acquired that status. This amendment, though a *volte face*, did not go far enough, however: the right to sponsor a spouse was still withheld from alien women and from those women who did not hold the new 'full' British citizenship which was to come into operation on 1st January 1983.

Many conservative backbenchers opposed the liberalisation, while the opposition decided to abstain, after they had argued initially that the liberalisation of the right to sponsor did not go far enough (Bhabha et al. 1985:67). Thus, the proposals were accepted.

However, as a result of the conservative backbench opposition against liberalisation and the resulting projected increase in immigration from the subcontinent, the Government introduced a few more safeguards, clearly the result of behind-the-scenes lobbying. When the new Rules were laid before Parliament on 6th December, still as HC 66, they contained, apart from the agreed liberalisation regarding the sponsoring of foreign husbands and fiancés, two additional rules to placate the anti-immigration lobby. These proposed changes must have been planned very carefully. They aroused real opposition and had, as we shall see, very wide-ranging implications. Firstly, the probationary period for marriages was extended to two years rather than one. Further, and more crucially, the burden of proof to show that the marriage was genuine and that it was not the primary purpose of the applicant to seek settlement in the UK was shifted to the applicant. There was also a much less noted indication that powers to deport men whose marriage to a British citizen had broken down would be increased (for details see Evans 1983:175 n.89).

Everybody was now upset, and the Government suffered an embarrassing defeat on 15th December 1982. On the one hand, many of its own supporters would not agree to the proposed extension of the right to sponsor a spouse to non-patrial British citizen women. In fact, backbench critics still demanded a total ban on the entry of husbands and fiancés, reminding the government of the day of the anti-immigration Election Manifesto of 1979; they also voiced their distrust of the ability to police the proposed new rules on marriages of convenience (Bevan 1986:267 n.74).

On the other hand, the extension of the probationary period to two years but even more the shifting of the burden of proof to the applicant were vigorously objected to by the opposition, presumably on grounds of expediency as much as in principle (see Bevan 1986:249).

Thus, the statement of changes to the Immigration Rules was not approved by Parliament and the Home Secretary was required to lay another statement within 40 days. In the meantime, HC 66 nevertheless came into effect unchanged on 1st January 1983; these Rules were to remain in force for a mere 46 days, till the coming into effect of HC 169, the important set of Immigration Rules of 16th February 1983.

Intense lobbying by the Government of its own right wing followed (see Bhabha et al. 1985:67) and HC 169 was laid before Parliament with some hurry (Marrington 1985:539), but important modifications which have been seen as an apparently liberal trade-off (Evans 1983:137). HC 169 retained the liberalised provisions of HC 66 on the rights of women to sponsor a husband or fiancé. The Rules now allowed all British citizen women with the right of abode to sponsor their spouse, thus excluding only certain female Commonwealth citizens and alien women. Of course, the rules were still discriminatory in terms of sex, since any man, irrespective of citizenship, and whether permanently settled in Britain or merely present for temporary purposes, remained eligible to be joined by his wife or fiancée (for details see Evans 1983:138).

The new Rules were also not in line with EEC law on the free movement rights of workers. In a very perceptive comment, Bhabha et al. (1985:68) stated:

'None of these restrictions applies to British men bringing over their wives. Neither do they apply to women who come over as workers from another EEC country. There is no sex discrimination under EEC immigration law, which allows all people from EEC member states who migrate in search of work to bring their families with them. This means that, in this respect, EEC women living in the UK are in a better position than British women.'

The only major change brought in by HC 169 related to the reduction of the probationary period, which was now again set at one year. This could be seen as a concession, but we already referred to the backbench view that this rule would not be effective anyway. So it would appear that the government now cleverly made a show of granting a concession, while in fact the really biting rule change, namely the shifting of the burden of proof to the male applicants, was retained from HC 66. All male applicants would now have 'the onerous task of proving a negative' (Marrington 1985:539), leading to the familiar no-win situation for spouses, with which immigration practitioners and their clients have had to struggle ever since.

There is no doubt that the British political establishment at this point decided to make full use of the discretionary powers of immigration officials. The ominous promise by the Government to its rebellious anti-immigration backbenchers that the new policy would be subject to continuous re-examination in the light of new circumstances (Bhabha et al. 1985:67) quite clearly did not indicate much willingness to place human rights concerns higher than British fears of being swamped.

Evans has argued that, at the end of the day, the addition of a few thousand husbands from the subcontinent should not have been a major consideration for introducing a system of immigration control that creates injustice and hardship, and which could not possibly be seen as conducive to good race relations:

'Whatever benefits the restrictions upon the entry and residence of foreign husbands produce, by assuring those concerned about the level of immigration from the New Commonwealth and Pakistan and the natural increase in the size of the black population (and this is what the Government appears to mean by 'improving race relations'), would seem to be more than offset by the hardships inflicted upon individuals, the indignities inherent in provisions that invite immigration officials to question people about intimate aspects of their personal lives, the opportunities for the arbitrary exercise of discretion that the Rules provide, and the sense of injustice likely to be created among the ethnic communities in Britain.' (Evans 1983:139-140).

It is apparent, thus, that pressure from Europe was a mixed blessing. Bevan (1986:254) saw the rule changes as,

'...a modest example of the effect of the European Convention on Human Rights. In context and retrospect, however, they are likely to be seen as a sordid episode in immigration history.'

The impending threat from European standards, then, did lead to a reluctant partial liberalisation of the sexually discriminatory rules, to be taken still further in 1985, after *Abdulaziz, Cabales and Balkandali* v. UK ([1985] 7 EHHR 471) had finally been decided. But the further development of the primary purpose rule under European pressure shows the exact opposite of liberalisation. This must have been felt quite strongly by activists at the time and is subtly indicated by Babha et al. (1985:76), concluding with some resignation that 'we are almost back to square one'.

☐ 3.5.3.4 The Immigration Rules of 1983 (HC 169)

As we saw in chapter 3.5.3.1, the new rule of HC 169 regarding the burden of proof to show that a marriage was not entered into with the primary purpose of settlement in Britain is not, in fact, totally new. It would appear that it merely legalises a pernicious practice that had been developed under cover for some time (see 3.5.3.1 above). By 1983, even if all other conditions were fulfilled, any male applicant's case could be refused on the basis of primary purpose. Thus, those in charge of British immigration control policies could afford to appear to give in quite generously on the sex discrimination front, while in reality the application of the new regime could now lead to as many refusals as one wanted.

The present section briefly outlines the set of Immigration Rules contained in HC 169. Though these Rules are no longer in force, it is relevant to look at them here since many important cases were decided under them and these particular Rules are important to show how the primary purpose rule has been developing further in this period.

We have seen that the Immigration Rules of H.C. 169, effective from 16th February 1983, retained or rather re-introduced the principle that all female British citizens are eligible to be joined by their husbands or fiancés. This human rights concession had to be made in view of the threats from Strasbourg (Macdonald and Blake 1991:260). At the same time, however, as Evans

(1983:137) and others have emphasised, the Government clearly intended to tighten the entry requirements further and found, as we saw, no difficulty in doing so. It is significant, looking at the structure of British immigration law, that these tightening mechanisms are not really found in the Rules themselves, but would become apparent only through the subsequent application of the Immigration Rules by immigration officials exercising their discretion against applicants rather than in their favour.

Here, then, is a major reason why the p.p.r. became, for the first time, such a centrally important instrument of British immigration control under HC 169. Despite the guarantee to female spouses of a right to sponsorship, the actual implementation of immigration control had to be geared towards continued exclusion of the maximum possible number of male applicants, especially from the Indian subcontinent, given that one wanted to keep the numbers of entrants to the UK from this part of the world as low as possible. Subsequent developments show how easy this has been for immigration officials, helped by the fact that H.C. 169 and subsequent Immigration Rules (now H.C. 251) have focused on the 'primary purpose' of such marriages.

The various subsequent developments contained within the 1983 Immigration Rules are of considerable importance, and are therefore discussed in some detail below. The provisions relating to fiancés in the Immigration Rules of 1983 (H.C.169) are found in Paragraph 41, which provides as follows:

'A man seeking to enter the United Kingdom for marriage to a woman settled here and who intends himself to settle thereafter should not be admitted unless he holds a current entry clearance granted to him for that purpose. An entry clearance will be refused unless the entry clearance officer is satisfied:

(a)   that it is not the primary purpose of the intended marriage to obtain admission to the United Kingdom; and

(b)   that there is an intention that the parties to the marriage should live together permanently as man and wife; and

(c)   that the parties to the proposed marriage have met.

Where the entry clearance officer is satisfied that all the conditions at (a) to (c) above apply, an entry clearance will, subject to the maintenance and accommodation requirements of this paragraph, be issued provided that the woman is a British citizen. An entry clearance should not be issued unless the entry clearance officer is satisfied that adequate maintenance and accommodation will be available for the fiancé until the date of his marriage, without the need to have recourse to public funds.'

In Paragraph 42 of H.C. 169, men holding an entry clearance issued under the preceding paragraphs were told that they should, subject to certain conditions, be admitted for three months and were advised to apply to the Home Office for an extension of stay once the marriage had taken place. A prohibition on employment during the three month period was also imposed by this para.

Interestingly, Paragraph 43 still makes special provisions for men seeking to enter the UK to marry a woman settled here, but indicating, at the same time, that they would after the marriage wish to settle overseas. Such applicants are to be admitted for three months, provided that the immigration officer is satisfied that the marriage will take place within a reasonable time, that the applicant and his spouse will leave the UK shortly after the marriage and that certain other requirements will be met. Rule 43 also enforces a prohibition on employment.

One could certainly not argue that Asian men are, in this case, treated unfairly or badly. For, the clear purpose of this rule is to facilitate the time-honoured customary arrangements among the various Asian communities that the responsibility for marriage arrangements falls upon the parents of the bride, who then have to let her go to the home of the husband. There can be no doubt that the British immigration authorities must have been more than happy with the continuation of such customary arrangements, for they led directly to a reduction in the numbers of young Asian women present in Britain, which has, of course, further implications for the Asian birthrate in the UK. At the same time, these superficially very considerate and lenient rules actually allow the Government not to concede anything at all in terms of immigration control.

Significantly, under these Rules, fiancées are not subject to any of the three requirements that govern male applicants. Paragraph 44 of HC 169 indicates concern only over whether the marriage will take place within a reasonable time and that adequate maintenance and accommodation will be provided to the applicant without recourse to public funds.

The provisions governing husbands under H.C. 169 are found in Paragraphs 54 and 55. Paragraph 54 states:

> 'The husband of a woman who is settled in the United Kingdom, or who is on the same occasion being admitted for settlement, is to be admitted if he holds a current entry clearance granted to him for that purpose. An entry clearance will be refused unless the entry clearance officer is satisfied:
>
> [a]   that the marriage was not entered into primarily to obtain admission to the United Kingdom; and
>
> [b]   that each of the parties has the intention of living permanently with the other as his or her spouse; and
>
> [c]   that the parties to the marriage have met.
>
> Where the entry clearance officer is satisfied that all the conditions at [a] to [c] above apply, an entry clearance will be issued provided that the wife is a British citizen. '

Paragraph 55 says in essence that a husband who holds an entry clearance issued under para 54 should, subject to certain requirements, be admitted for an initial period of up to 12 months and seems to indicate that leave to enter shall not be refused on grounds of restricted returnability or on medical grounds. There are four further paragraphs relating to marriage which govern eventualities that appear not important in the present context.

The rules regarding extension of stay for fiancés and husbands are found in Paragraphs 125 and 126 of HC 169. Here again, the dominant requirement is likely to be that the Secretary of State must be satisfied that it is not the primary purpose of the applicant to obtain settlement in the UK. Paragraph 125 provides:

> 'Fiancés arriving with entry clearance for the purpose of marriage to a woman settled here are normally admitted for 3 months. Subject to paragraph 126, if the marriage takes place within that period the man's stay should be extended for a further period not exceeding 12 months. Where an extension is granted any prohibition on the taking of employment should be removed and, subject to paragraph 126, the time limit should be removed at the end of that period. If the marriage does not take place within the initial 3 months an extension of stay is to be granted only if good cause is shown for the delay and there is satisfactory evidence that the marriage will take place at an early date thereafter. Subject to paragraph 126, a man who was admitted for a limited period as the husband of a woman settled here may have the time limit removed at the end of that period.'

The final sentence of this paragraph mentions those husbands that have originally been admitted in a temporary capacity and are virtually 'on probation'. They are now subjected to the primary purpose test for a second time. Paragraph 126 provides:

> 'Where a man admitted in temporary capacity marries a woman settled here, an extension of stay or leave to remain will not be granted, nor will any time limit on stay be removed, unless the Secretary of State is satisfied:
>
> (a)   that the marriage was not entered into primarily to obtain settlement here; and
>
> (b)   that the parties to the marriage have met; and
>
> (c)   that the husband has not remained in breach of the immigration laws before the marriage; and
>
> (d)   that the marriage has not taken place after a decision has been made to deport him or he has been recommended for deportation or been given notice under section 6(2) of the Immigration Act 1971; and
>
> (e)   that the marriage has not been terminated; and
>
> (f)   that each of the parties has the intention of living permanently with the other as his or her spouse.
>
> Where the Secretary of State is satisfied that all the conditions of (a) to (f) above apply, the husband will be allowed to remain, for 12 months in the first instance, provided that the wife is a British citizen. At the end of the 12 months' period the time limit on the husband's stay may, subject to (a) to (f) above, be removed.'

We see here that the new Rules are imposing a number of additional requirements on husbands seeking extension of stay, with particular concern shown about any breaches of immigration law committed by the man during his period of probation. While the focus appears to be on weeding out those men who entered into marriages of convenience of one kind or another, little is made here of the primary purpose rule. This low-key approach in the wording of the Rules themselves, however, should not deceive us into thinking that the p.p.r. was not a central consideration.

Macdonald (1987:234) seems to say that the p.p.r. is distinct from the marriage of convenience rule (see also now Macdonald and Blake 1991:260-261). This is true from the legal point of view. It could be argued, however, that the suspicion that many Asian marriages are primarily entered into to obtain settlement in the UK and that there may not even be any intention to live permanently together as husband and wife must have significantly contributed to the development of the p.p.r. as it now appears.

The rephrasing of the Rules also involved some procedural changes. Among them, as we saw already, the shift in the onus of proof is certainly most important. Under the pre-1983 law the Secretary of State had to satisfy the Immigration Appeal Tribunal that:

> 'First of all, the marriage is entered into for the primary purpose of evading the immigration law and rules, and, second, the necessity of there being no intention, or a lack of intention to live together permanently as man and wife.' (Per Lord Lane L.C.J. in *Mahmud Khan* (1983) QB 79O, at 793).

Similar comments have been made in *Anseereeganoo* (1981) Imm AR 3O and *Class-Peter* (1981) Imm AR 154. Under HC 169, however, the burden of proof lies on the entrant. This gives the Home Office a double chance of success illustrated, for example, by a comparison of the unreported cases of *Tanveer* (3456) and *Bhatia* (3456). The Junior Home Office Minister in an interview on the Channel 4 programme 'Eastern Eye' on 10th January 1984 regarded the then current test as 'perfectly easy to apply'. In Parliament, (*H.C. Debates* [18 November 1982], col.238) he re-iterated the procedure:

> 'A husband or fiancé overseas is interviewed in every case before an entry clearance is granted. In many cases his wife or fiancée here is also interviewed. An application has to be made in every case before a husband is granted settlement, and he and his wife will be interviewed wherever there is cause to doubt the bona fides of the application. Home Office staff and interviewing officers who are experienced in assessing applicants, take into consideration not only the statements of the applicant, his spouse, and of third parties, but also the applicant's immigration history and other relevant information to establish whether the requirements in the rules are satisfied.' (quoted by Bevan 1986:250).

This description makes the interview procedure seem relatively straightforward. In fact, however, it is known that the procedures on the admission of husbands and fiancés are far from simple. Newdick (1985:816) has rightly pointed out that 'discovering the nature of a person's motives for behaviour is notoriously difficult'. There can be no doubt that the shift in the onus of proof 'has more than counterbalanced the more liberal aspects of the 1983 Rules' (Bevan 19836:249).

☐ 3.5.3.5 The full-fledged application of the primary purpose rule after 1983

The outwardly minor and almost cosmetic changes to the Immigration Rules in 1983 should not deceive anyone into thinking that life had now become easier for Asian women in Britain and their spouses or fiancés overseas. The exact opposite was true; this was realised more or less immediately, as Bhabha et al. (1985:68) have made clear:

'It soon became evident that large numbers of British women were still being prevented from living in Britain with their foreign husbands, especially if the men came from the Indian subcontinent. The 'primary purpose' clause of the Rules is being operated much more stringently than in former years now...'

Now, even if a particular marriage was perfectly valid in law, it was not sufficient to satisfy immigration officers that the parties intended their marriage to last forever, or had already been married for a considerable time and might even have children. Thus:

'Even where it is quite clear that a marriage is 'genuine' in this sense, husbands are refused entry if it is suspected that their main motive for getting married is to live in the UK.' (Bhabha et al. 1985:68).

The same authors (1985:68-69) show that the anti-immigration lobby in Parliament monitored the progress of the primary purpose rule very closely and was putting constant pressure on the Home Secretary to ensure that the figures for the admission of spouses from the subcontinent did not go up significantly. Indeed, despite the so-called liberalisation of the Rules in February 1983, which had clearly led to an increase in applications from 1,230 in 1982 to 3,300 in 1983, only 1,080 applications were granted in 1983 as opposed to 800 in 1982, an increase of merely 280 persons.

The statistics from this time reveal the gradually more stringent application of the primary purpose rule in two other ways. Firstly, the refusal rate of applications by husbands and fiancés shows a continuous upward trend since 1977, when such figures began to be collected (see Bhabha et al. 1985:69):

1977	4.0%	1981	10.0%
1978	6.0%	1982	47.0%
1979	8.0%	1983	47.0%
1980	9.0%		

This column of figures would seem to indicate quite clearly that already prior to the official introduction of the primary purpose rule under HC 169, officials had, as it were, experimented with a higher overall refusal rate, obviously also in an attempt to keep the figures of successful applications as low as possible. But they were at the same time, one could argue, testing the scope for official discretion. We shall see in the next chapter that this policy, more or less inevitably, had to lead to the growth of case-law, and the resulting shift of the focus of British immigration control to the arena of the courts rather than Parliament or the Home Secretary's offices. Since the more or less unbridled discretion of immigration officials would not be acceptable to many lawyers, we shall see how British immigration law rapidly established itself as a separate and important branch of law, with a heavy and continuous input to the higher courts' workload on judicial review (see Griffith 1991:13 and Ian Macdonald's ILPA lecture at Vol.2 No.3 [October 1987] of *Immigration and Nationality Law and Practice*, pp. 54-59, at p. 56). More recently, this has attracted adverse comments and new apprehensions (see Scannell 1992).

A further indication of purposeful tightening of the primary purpose rule in this period is provided by evidence collected by Bhabha et al. (1985:69). They showed that while the overall refusal rate for husbands and fiancés in 1982 and 1983 remained the same at 47 %, the reasons for refusal have been shifting:

> 'Home Office figures reveal a dramatic increase in the proportion of applications turned down partly or wholly on the grounds that the 'primary purpose' of the marriage was immigration to Britain — from 18 per cent in 1982 to 73 per cent in 1983.'

This, then, confirms quite clearly that the primary purpose rule became, especially since 1983 and after HC 169, the major device by which immigration officials would hold back the imagined flood of male applicants from the Indian subcontinent. Bhabha et al. (1985:69-70) have shown how the Home Office was trying to deny this, while there was new evidence at the same time, collected by the Joint Council for the Welfare of Immigrants, that doubtful cases were now no longer referred to the Home Office for further consideration but were decided on the spot. In practice, quite obviously, the primary purpose rule 'is now central to the rules on admission and settlement for marriage' (Macdonald 1987:231).

This development has, quite clearly, further increased the discretion of immigration officials, especially of entry clearance officers at the critical overseas posts, who were given new secret instructions after the 1983 Rules came into force that allowed them (or probably required them) to use intensive interrogation of applicants and their sponsors. This was coupled with instructions to exercise discretion in a negative way, i.e., not to give the benefit of the doubt to applicants (Bhabha et al. 1985:70).

Such official guidance from the top 'inevitably influences the attitudes and judgements of individual immigration officers' (Bhabha et al. 1985:70) and therefore helped further to institutionalise the British system of immigration control with its specifically designed focus on keeping non-white people out of the country. It is not surprising that, apart from the European challenge, this policy would not find universal approval within Britain and would be challenged in a variety of ways.

☐ 3.5.3.6 The rule changes of 1985 (HC 503)

Before turning to the case-law on primary purpose, we now briefly consider the impact of the final decision by the European Court of Human Rights in *Abdulaziz, Cabales and Balkandali* v. *UK*, reported at [1985] 7 EHRR 471 on the further development of the primary purpose rule in Britain.

Writing before the European Court of Human Rights had come up with its final decision in this case on 28th May 1985, Evans (1983:140-141) rehearsed the potential arguments of the British government in defence of its then current regime of immigration controls regarding spouses and fiancés. He first identified economic arguments, in particular the strong economic motive that many men may have for seeking to stay in the UK and the adverse effect that this might have on the UK labour market, a frequently advanced reasoning that can be shown to be quite misguided (see Simon 1989 for the USA). Evans (1983:141) also argued that the preferential treatment of a substantial number of non-citizens with only a grandparental connection would have implications on the labour market, too, thus weakening the UK's labour market argument.

Next, Evans focused on the arguments concerning racial or ethnic discrimination, which he thought the British government would refute rather easily by recourse to the rejoinder that it was entitled to develop objective criteria for classifying persons who should fall under immigration control, that so doing was in fact good for race relations, and that, at any rate, international law gave national laws the final say over immigration control (Evans 1983:140-141). The same argument would be used to defend the charge of unlawful restrictions of the right to family life. Further, devices to control arranged marriages could be seen as necessary to prevent the evasion of control and it would probably be argued that 'this method of selecting marriage partners does not accord with the widely shared social customs and values of British society' (Evans 1983:141).

Finding that the British Government was not immune from challenge despite some changes to the Rules, Evans then put his own views against the above arguments. He showed, first of all, that the labour force argument, in view of evidence of a higher participation rate of women and official encouragement of gender equality in employment, could equally be applied to immigrant women. Indeed, one could argue, this line of reasoning would support a total ban on immigration to Britain.

Further, Evans (1983:141) opposed the notion that regardless of circumstances, a woman should normally be expected to live in her husband's country of origin, which seemed to him 'quite at odds with contemporary social norms', a view supported by reference to rule changes in British nationality law that reduced gender discrimination. Rather, he saw unjustifiable restrictions on the right to marry and to family life, affecting mainly persons of non-European origin, particularly men from the Indian subcontinent (Evans 1983:142). He also found himself unable to support the view that the racially discriminatory restrictions against parties to all arranged marriages were in fact hitting all such parties, since more prosperous people could afford to comply more easily with the requirement to have met. Nor was such discriminatory treatment needed to weed out bogus marriages; this was already achieved by paragraph 54 [b] of HC 169, requiring that each of the parties must have the intention of living permanently with the other as his or her spouse. Evans (1982:142) also criticised the latitude given to immigration officials to scrutinise the parties' marital relationship, which would again particularly hit Asian couples.

However, while all these arguments are certainly helpful and appropriate, it is significant that they overlook the actual application of the primary purpose rule after the onus of proof had been shifted to the applicant. Now, whatever evidence one provided as an applicant might still not satisfy immigration officers. How could this be challenged? The fact that this particular question did not arise in the chain of arguments provided by Evans may indicate how successful the government was at first in hiding its invidious use of the primary purpose rule.

It appears that Bevan (1986:248-249), writing a little later, took the argument slightly further by using the principle of proportionality argument more explicitly, though he too did not apply it to the primary purpose rule itself. His argument, in view of the 1980 Rules, related to the proviso that a sponsoring woman or one of her parents must have been born in the UK. If this rule was designed to weed out exploitation of marriage as a means to settlement, it could be seen as superfluous and disproportionately onerous, since other parts of the same Rules took care of that already (Bevan 1986:248). But Bevan did not take that argument any further.

In Strasbourg, as anticipated by Evans (1983:140), the UK government sought to defend its restrictions on the entry rights of husbands and fiancés and the more favourable treatment given to female applicants primarily by economic arguments. The reasoning was, basically, that male immigrants contributed to the workforce, had clear economic motivations for wishing to come to Britain and were, therefore, marrying British women because of the economic benefits (see also Bhabha et al. 1985:63). They were thus hidden primary migrants, which led Bhabha et al. (1985:63) to comment with some indignation that women were somehow seen as secondary yet again.

This rather one-sided economic argumentation overlooks, and quite purposely, the emotional and cultural elements involved in the Asian arranged marriage system. If British Asian women were not to marry South Asian men, whom could they marry? If the law made it easy for British Asian men to bring in spouses from the subcontinent, there would be few marriageable Asian men left in Britain. The alternatives for British Asian women were — and are today — quite startling: agree to be virtually repatriated or at least removed from the UK by marrying a South Asian man from anywhere in the world, marry 'out of caste' in the UK, or remain unmarried. The official assumption appears to have been that less and less South Asians would actually wish to arrange intercontinental marriages. This feeling was apparently shared by some writers. Evans (1983: 139-140) argued that 'as the ethnic communities' ties with their countries of origin weaken, more women will marry men who are already here.' In other words, there was a perception that the problem would go away over time. But this has not, so far, been the case in many communities, though there clearly are significant differences among diferent Asian communities which cannot be explored here.

The European Court of Human Rights in Strasbourg, deciding three test cases of women from Britain who had not been allowed to be joined by their husbands, found unanimously that there had not been a violation of Article 8, the right to respect for family life, since there was no obligation on contracting states to respect the choice by married couples of the country of their residence. This, in the light of earlier decisions (see above, p.80) was an expected and negative result.

Next, the Court turned to Article 14, under which the question arose whether the 1980 Immigration Rules were discriminatory on the basis of sex. Here the Court accepted, in principle, the UK Government's argument that the 1980 Rules had the legitimate aim of protecting the domestic labour market. But it was held, nevertheless, that the United Kingdom had not advanced weighty enough reasons to differentiate between men and women, nor was the argument of promoting public tranquillity taken as sufficiently weighty to justify stricter immigration controls for men than for women. It was, thus, unanimously held that the three applicants had been victims of discrimination on the grounds of sex, contrary to Article 14 together with Article 8 (see Berger 1989:295).

Significantly, the Court did not produce a finding that there had been discrimination on the ground of race, nor of birth, nor had there been inhuman and degrading treatment, though the applicants were awarded costs.

The UK, thus, got away lightly, but this case made it necessary for Britain to develop a new set of Immigration Rules that would put male and female applicants on an equal footing when it came to sponsoring a spouse for entry or settlement in the UK. There was considerable speculation about what the UK would do in response. The official reaction came, as Marrington (1985:543-544) has written, 'as an unpleasant surprise to even the most seasoned immigration watchers'.

The Home Secretary laid a new set of Immigration Rules (HC 503) before Parliament on 15th July 1985. These Rules came into force on 26th August 1985. The most significant element in them is the 'levelling down' of standards, with the effect that now any man or woman could seek to sponsor a spouse, but all applicants were made subject to more stringent requirements, including of course the primary purpose test, but now subject also to more stringent maintenance and accommodation requirements that have become much more central to British immigration control recently (Gillespie 1992).

Since in the meantime the primary purpose rule had been further developed and fine-tuned, with great effectiveness in terms of immigration control, it would seem that there was not much need for official panic. By 1985 Britain already had what many politicians and their electorate wanted, namely a racially discriminatory and openly exclusionary system that purported to achieve formal equality, but in effect excluded whole classes of people at will. David Marrington's summing up of the 1985 Immigration Rules is a telling comment:

'In sum, the new immigration rules are a striking example of the substantive injustice that can be achieved under the guise of formal equality. Although apparently responding to a justified demand for an end to sex discrimination in immigration law, the new provisions are not only inconsistent with the spirit of the European Court's judgement, they are also an affront to the right to family life enshrined in the Convention itself.' (Marrington 1985:544).

HC 503, with effect from 26th August 1985, first of all entitled all women settled in the UK to be joined by their partners from anywhere in the world, so that the rules for the admission and settlement of husbands/wives and fiancés/fiancées are now the same. This sounds good and liberal, but this new entitlement is, of course, subject to a range of stringent requirements, so that in effect the relaxation of a restriction is immediately counterbalanced by the effects of a whole string of new qualifications found in this set of Immigration Rules.

The substantive provisions with which we are concerned here are difficult to locate, since HC 503 is phrased in the nature of amendments to HC 169 of 1983 and not as a new set of Immigration Rules in its own right. It is immediately obvious, however, that the majority of provisions contained in the eight printed pages of HC 503 is focused on spouses, fiancés and fiancées. Macdonald (1987:520-569) provides full coverage of HC 169 in its original and amended forms.

Apart from the explicit focus on spouses in HC 503, several provisions centre on public funds and the maintenance and accommodation requirements. Lawrence Grant (1987) has discussed these in considerable detail and we can be fairly brief here. Thus, para 1 of HC 503 provides clarification to the effect that the term 'public funds' means 'Supplementary Benefit, Housing Benefit, Family Income Supplement and housing under the Housing (Homeless Persons) Act 1977'. Para 6 of HC 503 adds a new para 15A to paragraph 15 of HC 169, relating to provisions for a relative or friend of a person seeking entry to the UK. Such friend or relative may be asked to give a written undertaking 'to be responsible for that person's maintenance and accommodation for the period of any leave granted, including any variation'. Corresponding provisions are made for persons seeking variation of leave under para 17 of HC 503, which inserts a new para 94A into paragraph 94 of HC 169.

Such provisions are a clear indication that only applicants with connections and with contact persons in the UK willing to sign the required documents will be given entry clearance, even for temporary purposes. These rules affect, therefore, visitors just as much as spouses and fiancés, and they have certainly had the effect of increasing the refusal rates for visitor visa applications by young people of less affluent backgrounds. Thus, here are rather indirect and wide-ranging control mechanisms designed to repel even potential spouses, with the effect that access to the UK is now also being denied to many perfectly genuine visitors. These might be persons seeking to visit relatives, but frequently they could be tourists without contacts or potential sponsors in the UK so could be refused entry clearance for being unable to provide the undertaking required in the new paragraph 15A.

It would be inappropriate here to comment in detail on the detrimental economic side-effects of this rule for the UK. The size of the Indian middle classes today is estimated at well over 100 million people (with a total Indian population of now almost 850 million), so the UK is clearly and foolishly depriving itself of a large pool of foreign tourists, who now go instead to Singapore, Hong Kong and other places for their shopping and sightseeing, since 'Fortress Europe' simply cannot imagine that whole plane loads of South Asians would just want to come as tourists. Presumably, such assumptions are never applied to Japanese tourists, whose presence in Britain is not immediately linked with immigration phobias.

The most important provisions of HC 503 for our present purpose are found in paragraphs 8, 10 and 22. Paragraph 8 provides that paras 41-44 of HC 169 are to be replaced by the new paragraphs 41 and 42 of HC 503 regarding fiancés and fiancées. Paragraph 41 of HC 503 is most relevant and reads as follows:

'A passenger seeking admission to the United Kingdom for marriage to a person present and settled in the United Kingdom or who is on the same occasion being admitted for settlement, and who intends to settle thereafter must hold a current entry clearance granted for that purpose. An entry clearance will be refused unless the entry clearance officer is satisfied:-

(a)   that it is not the primary purpose of the intended marriage to obtain admission to the United Kingdom; and

(b)   that there is an intention that the parties to the marriage should live together permanently as man and wife; and

(c)   that the parties to the proposed marriage have met;

(d)   that adequate maintenance and accommodation without recourse to public funds will be available for the applicant until the date of the marriage; and

(e)   (i) that there will thereafter be adequate accommodation for the parties and their dependents without recourse to public funds in accommodation of their own or which they occupy themselves; and
(ii) that the parties will thereafter be able to maintain themselves and their dependents adequately without recourse to public funds.'

We see here the exemplary use of non-sexist language, such as 'passenger', not 'man', a toning down of the rather negative and confrontational wording of the old paragraph 41, but no change in substance other than the removal of gender discrimination in these Rules. Regarding the conditions that applicants have to satisfy, (a) to (c) remain unchanged, but the accommodation and maintenance requirements have now been upgraded to the status of full conditions. This would also mean that the burden of proof regarding these conditions rests now definitely on the applicant, a further high hurdle, since the conditions in (e) relate to future arrangements, of which many applicants will not be certain at the time of applying for entry clearance. As we shall see in the case-law, this has indeed given rise to new problems in legal practice. The problems were wisely anticipated by Jim Gillespie (1986:23-24) who alerted advisors to the new pitfalls on public funds.

Paragraph 42 of HC 169 is only modified by HC 503 to the effect that 'passenger' replaces 'man', while the old para 44 is now redundant, since fiancées are also covered by the new paragraphs 41 and 42.

Interestingly, Paragraph 43 of HC 169, which made special provisions for men seeking to enter the UK temporarily to marry a woman settled here has now been taken out of the Rules. One may presume that such cases would now be covered by the new paragraph 41 of HC 503, since a man seeking admission to the UK only for the purpose of celebrating his marriage in Britain would then not be able to apply later to the Home Office for an extension of stay leading to permanent settlement. It would probably be correct to assume that a stated change of purpose of the husband at the time of seeking an extension would be squarely hit by the primary purpose rule and by the new provisions of paragraphs 97-100 under HC 503.

Paragraph 10 of HC 503 amalgamates the new non-discriminatory provisions governing spouses which were found under paras 46-49 and 54-55 of HC 169 in the two new paragraphs 46-47. Paragraph 46 states:

> 'A passenger seeking admission to the United Kingdom as the spouse of a person who is present and settled in the United Kingdom, or who is on the same occasion being admitted for settlement, must hold a current entry clearance granted for that purpose. An entry clearance will be refused unless the entry clearance officer is satisfied:-
>
> (a) that the marriage was not entered into primarily to obtain admission to the United Kingdom; and
>
> (b) that each of the parties has the intention of living permanently with the other as his or her spouse; and
>
> (c) that the parties to the marriage have met; and
>
> (d) that there will be adequate accommodation for the parties and their dependents without recourse to public funds in accommodation of their own or which they occupy themselves; and
>
> (e) that the parties will be able to maintain themselves and their dependents adequately without recourse to public funds.'

The new paragraph 47 of HC 503 says in essence that a passenger holding an entry clearance issued under para 46 should, subject to certain requirements, be admitted for an initial period of up to 12 months.

The major change here is again the introduction of the maintenance and accommodation requirements for spouses on top of the familiar qualifications under (a) to (c). This new situation will now give rise to refusals of applications on multiple grounds so that, at least in theory, fewer rejections may be made on the basis of primary purpose alone. This rule change could, therefore, be exploited to produce statistics that show no increase in the proportion of applications refused on the basis of primary purpose.

Paragraph 22 of HC 503 replaces paras 123-126 of HC 169 with new paras 123-125. These rules concern extensions of stay and again subject applicants to the primary purpose test at this stage. The new paragraph 123 reads as follows:

> 'Fiancés and fiancées arriving with entry clearances for the purpose of marriage to a person settled here are normally admitted for 3 months. If the marriage does not take place within the initial 3 months, an extension of stay subject to a prohibition on employment is to be granted only if good cause is shown for the delay and there is satisfactory evidence that the marriage will take place at an early date and that the maintenance and accommodation requirements in paragraph 41 continue to be met. If the marriage does take place an application for extension of stay on the basis of the marriage is to be considered under paragraph 124.'

Paragraph 123 clearly indicates that persons who have been admitted for three months for the purpose of marriage to a partner settled in the UK may be granted an extension of stay. But this is made subject to a prohibition on employment, proof of impending marriage arrangements and now also stringent maintenance and accommodation requirements. At this stage, it would appear, the primary purpose rule does not come into play directly, though delaying tactics by the applicant would probably be interpreted as evidence of *mala fides* and could increase the likelihood of refusal under paragraph 124.

Paragraph 123 represents certainly a tightening up of the rules for fiancés and fiancées and indicates a much less sympathetic approach to applicants through the changed wording. This particular rule appears to have caused some administrative problems, which were sought to be alleviated by amendments to this paragraph in 1988. The amended rules were laid before Parliament on 14th December 1987 and came into effect on 1st February 1988 (see Marrington 1988:463). Their effect was to grant fiancés and fiancées an initial period of six rather than three months, at the end of which the provisions for extension of stay in paragraph 124 would apply. Marrington (1988:464) has argued that this may well have been a labour-saving device for the Home Office, but these rule changes were introduced in conjunction with amended visitor rules, which were almost clandestinely restricting visitor visas to a maximum of six months, thus making extended family visits problematic.

The new paragraph 124 in HC 503 has also become a central plank of British immigration control at the stage of extension of stay. The paragraph reads as follows:

'Where a person with limited leave seeks an extension of stay on the basis of marriage to a person settled here, an extension will not be granted unless the Secretary of State is satisfied:

(a)   that the marriage was not entered into primarily to obtain settlement here; and

(b)   that the parties to the marriage have met; and

(c)   that the applicant has not remained in breach of the immigration laws; and

(d)   that the marriage has not taken place after a decision has been made to deport him or he has been recommended for deportation or been given notice under section 6(2) of the Immigration Act 1971; and

(e)   that the marriage has not been terminated; and

(f)   that each of the parties has the intention of living permanently with the other as his or her spouse; and

(g)   that there will be adequate accommodation for the parties and their dependents without recourse to public funds in accommodation of their own or which they occupy themselves; and

(h)   that the parties will be able to maintain themselves and their dependents adequately without recourse to public funds.

When the Secretary of State is satisfied that all the conditions at (a) to (h) above apply, the applicant will be allowed to remain, for 12 months in the first instance.'

In addition, paragraph 125 of HC 503 provides the relevant rules for the final hurdle to be taken by spouses:

'A person who was admitted for a limited period, or given an extension of stay, as the spouse of a person settled here may have the time limit on their stay removed at the end of that period if the Secretary of State is satisfied that the marriage has not been terminated and that each of the parties has the intention of living permanently with the other as his or her spouse.'

We see here that the new Rules are imposing a number of additional requirements on husbands and wives seeking an extension of stay or permanent settlement. Particular concern is again shown about the maintenance and accommodation requirements, which are now an integral part of all the relevant Rules. Further, as Ian Macdonald (1987:233) emphasised as the most notable differences of the new Rules, any breaches of immigration law committed by the applicant during the period of probation will weigh heavily against the applicant, who still has to show that the marriage was not entered into primarily to obtain settlement in the UK and that it is a genuine and lasting marital union. The process of weeding out those men, in particular, who might have entered into marriages of convenience of one kind or another continues here. The Rules themselves do not make it clear how important this aspect is in relation to others, nor do they state how central the primary purpose rule is in practice, though it tops the list of conditions, of course. All we see, from the Rules themselves, is that all the stipulated conditions have to be satisfied before any entry clearance or settlement right is given. This is a tall order indeed. But it was quite certainly not the only purpose of the amendments in HC 503 to make the existing regime sexually non-discriminatory: the fresh opportunity to introduce yet more hurdles was used with some circumspection.

Comments on the new set of Rules by writers are not very detailed, though Macdonald's second edition (Macdonald 1987), Mole (1987), the detailed article by Lawrence Grant (1987) and a number of other texts are based on the then current set of Rules. Mostly, writers have confined themselves to re-stating the rules and their major effects for the practical purposes of immigration advisers.

Jim Gillespie (1986), in the very first issue of *Immigration and Nationality Law and Practice*, pointing out that there were not yet any decisions under the new set of Rules, provided a helpful overview of the changes from the Home Office perspective, based on first-hand knowledge. He also notes that many transitional provisions and savings applied, so that not all new applications would be governed by the new restrictive regime of HC 503 (Gillespie 1986:23). He confirms that the issue of public funds has acquired a higher profile among the concerns of the Home Office and is administered in three ways: by the definition of 'public funds' for the first time, by making more categories of applicants (in particular now husbands) subject to the maintenance and accommodation requirements, and by the greater use of sponsors' declarations (Gillespie 1986:23).

It is relevant to point out here how the public funds issue could be linked with the question of 'primary purpose' (see e.g. Sondhi 1987:77-78). Gillespie showed that male applicants who had arranged employment in the UK and were thus safe from the public funds hurdle, would risk falling foul of the primary purpose hurdle, since entry clearance officers had been instructed by the Home Office 'that pre-arranged employment is a factor to be taken into account in assessing the primary purpose of an intended marriage' (Gillespie 1986:24). On the other hand, entry clearance officers had also been instructed to ascertain the employment prospects of applicants, so that an applicant who was only able to express vague aspirations would also be in danger of refusal.

Otherwise, Gillespie (1986:24) seemed to think that the new Rules 'pose few problems of interpretation' but that their application by the Home Office would tighten up on people who made 'declarations' that might later be shown to be doubtful (Gillespie 1986:25), pointing to the increasingly important issue of credibility of applicants and sponsors, which arose from the now institutionalised process of intensive interviewing (see Newdick 1985:817).

Nuala Mole, clearly concerned that good immigration advisers should ensure that their clients were not refused the first time round (Mole 1987:4), raised another important issue when she advised that it was preferable if the applicants were married rather than merely engaged:

'In practice it is far more difficult to satisfy an ECO of both the primary purpose and the genuineness and permanence of a relationship which is still in an inchoate state. Advisers should make sure that clients are aware of this.' (Mole 1987:26-27).

This has clearly been of some importance in practice and it would be useful to have a detailed specialist study on this particular issue. From experience in the community, it is now quite apparent that Mole's advice was sound and appropriate. But the continuously high refusal rates for male spouses over many years have made many families in certain communities wary of full-fledged marriage arrangements till immigration clearance is secured. This is clearly a conundrum to which no solution can be offered. It may have the indirect effect, in the long run, that less Asian women will even contemplate marrying a man from the subcontinent — certainly a desired result of British immigration control and of the primary purpose rule, but achieved at the cost, as always in this context, of women's right to family life.

☐ 3.5.3.7 Recent developments: Fine-tuning exclusionary mechanisms

Further amendments to HC 169 were made from time to time between 1985 and 1988; details of most of these have been reported in an accessible form by Peter Moss (1988a;1988b) and Jim Gillespie (1990a;1990b), so we need not discuss them here in any depth. Also, none of the more recent rule changes specifically concerns the primary purpose rule, which is now firmly in place and need not be officially modified any longer, confirming the conclusion that,

'...it remains as true as ever that much of Home Office practice is contained not in the published immigration rules but rather in extra-statutory concessions. This puts considerable obstacles in the way of the unwary adviser seeking to give accurate advice.' (Gillespie 1990a:16).

Several of the recent changes related to spouses, bringing for example revised definitions of 'public funds' in HC 555 with effect from 1st August 1988. Earlier, a ban had been imposed on the entry of spouses below 16 years in HC 306 with effect from 23rd May 1986. This ban was made absolutely watertight by HC 555 on 1st August 1988, so one thought, since it now also covered those wives that were earlier explicitly protected by section 1(5) of the *Immigration Act*, 1971. However, on 23rd March 1990, when HC 251 came into force, a final turn was given to the restriction screw on under-age marriages, as we shall explain below. This rule change must have been stimulated by a mere handful of cases, but it shows how much attention the Home Office has been willing to give to watertight exclusionary mechanisms.

A brief comparison of the revised and the new rule will illustrate this point. Paragraph 1A of HC 169, inserted into the Rules by HC 306 with effect from 23rd May 1986, provided as follows:

'1A. Nothing in these rules shall be construed as permitting a person (other than a person referred to in section 1(5) of the Immigration Act 1971) to be granted entry clearance, leave to enter or remain or variation of leave as a spouse of another if he or she will be aged under 16 at the date of arrival in the UK or (as the case may be) on the date on which the leave to remain or variation of leave is granted.'

This rule, which still allowed entry to the UK to spouses of Commonwealth citizens settled here before 1st January 1973, was then amended by HC 555, as indicated above. The new wording of what is now paragraph 2 in HC 251 of 23rd March 1990 is:

'2. Nothing in these rules shall be construed as permitting a person to be granted entry clearance, leave to enter or remain or variation of leave as a spouse of another if either party to the marriage will be aged under 16 at the date of arrival in the United Kingdom or (as the case may be) on the date on which the leave to remain or variation of leave is granted.'

The effect of this rule change is that entry is now prohibited also in cases where the spouse in the UK is below 16 years of age. Thus, as Jim Gillespie (1990b:75) explained,

'Where a 15-year-old Pakistani girl (with a right to settle in the UK) is married to a 21-year-old Pakistani man the husband will not now be able to qualify for entry clearance until the wife reaches the age of 16.'

This series of small changes must obviously be seen as a reaction to the continued practice of child marriage in the subcontinent and, in fact, in Britain (see Poulter 1986:16-22). It may, therefore, be welcomed in principle.

However, such rule changes must also be understood in the light of the *Immigration Act* of 1988. This brief Act constituted, *inter alia,* a concerted attack on the cultural traditions of Britain's immigrant communities and was widely perceived to discriminate on grounds of race (Blake and Scannell 1988) because it took away, as we saw above, the explicit guarantee of the right to family life for male Commonwealth citizens settled in Britain on 1st January 1973.

It would therefore seem that the 1988 Act and the Rules made after it focused in an almost obsessive manner on small groups of potential immigrants, such as the 70 or so polygamously married women who might annually come to join husbands in Britain. As Moss (1988:54) explains, HC 555 of 1st August 1988 consequently banned the entry of polygamously married wives to the UK, even if the woman in question had a right of abode, where a co-wife was already present in the UK. There were some saving provisions (see Moss 1988:54), but the trend towards exclusionary practices is further strengthened. Paragraph 3 of HC 251 in 1990 has reinforced this rule and contains the current law.

There is remarkably little coverage about the introduction of the current set of Immigration Rules, HC 251 in 1990. As noted, these Rules were laid before

Parliament on 23rd March 1990 and came into effect that very day, not necessitated by great urgency, but by all-party agreement, it would appear, that a consolidation of the by now very messy system of HC 169 with its manifold amendments would be desirable.

Gillespie (1990b) has briefly reviewed the major changes introduced by HC 251. His coverage shows that the primary purpose rule was not a relevant factor in these rule changes. In fact, compared to the 1983 Rules of H.C. 169, the marriage rules have only seen some minor adjustments, which explains why the most recent textbooks like Macdonald and Blake (1991) do not cover them in detail and can focus on the case-law instead.

This situation further illustrates the point made by Jim Gillespie (see above, p.100) that British immigration control is now achieved not so much by changes to the relevant statute, nor even the Immigration Rules (on this see now Vincenzi and Marrington 1992), but by administrative instructions which are able to by-pass parliamentary control. Thus, in 1992, we are still governed by the *Immigration Act* of 1971, despite very considerable changes to British immigration law since then. Further, even the most recent full set of Immigration Rules could afford simply to re-state the earlier position regarding the entry and settlement of spouses. The real controlling process, the day-to-day fine-tuning, as it were, takes place outside the Rules, through communications to immigration officers from the Home Office.

The relevant Rules of HC 251 for the admission of fiancés, fiancées and spouses in paragraphs 47-48 and 50-51 respectively, together with the rules regarding extensions in paragraphs 130-132 now read as follows:

'Fiancés and fiancées

47. A passenger seeking admission to the United Kingdom for marriage to a person present and settled in the United Kingdom or who is on the same occasion being admitted for settlement, and who intends to settle thereafter must hold a current entry clearance granted for that purpose. An entry clearance will be refused unless the entry clearance officer is satisfied:

(a) that it is not the primary purpose of the intended marriage to obtain admission to the United Kingdom; and

(b) that there is an intention that the parties to the marriage should live together permanently as husband and wife; and

(c) that the parties to the proposed marriage have met; and

(d) that adequate maintenance and accommodation without recourse to public funds will be available for the applicant until the date of the marriage; and

(e) (i) that there will thereafter be adequate accommodation for the parties and their dependents without recourse to public funds in accommodation of their own or which they occupy themselves; and (ii) that the parties will thereafter be able to maintain themselves and their dependents adequately without recourse to public funds.

48. A passenger holding an entry clearance issued under the preceding paragraph should, subject to paragraph 17, be admitted for 6 months and advised to apply to the Home Office once the marriage has taken place for an extension of stay. A prohibition on employment should be imposed.

Spouses

50. A passenger seeking admission to the United Kingdom as the spouse of a person who is present and settled in the United Kingdom, or who is on the same occasion being admitted for settlement, must hold a current entry clearance granted for that purpose. An entry clearance will be refused unless the entry clearance officer is satisfied:

(a)   that the marriage was not entered into primarily to obtain admission to the United Kingdom; and

(b)   that each of the parties has the intention of living permanently with the other as his or her spouse; and

(c)   that the parties to the marriage have met; and

(d)   that there will be adequate accommodation for the parties and their dependents without recourse to public funds in accommodation of their own or which they occupy themselves; and

(e)   that the parties will be able to maintain themselves and their dependents adequately without recourse to public funds

51. A passenger holding an entry clearance issued under the preceding paragraph should, subject to paragraph 17, be admitted for an initial period of up to 12 months.

Marriage

130. Fiancés and fiancées arriving with entry clearances for the purpose of marriage to a person settled here are normally admitted for 6 months. If the marriage does not take place within the initial 6 months, an extension of stay subject to a prohibition on employment is to be granted only if good cause is shown for the delay and and there is satisfactory evidence that the marriage will take place at an early date and that the maintenance and accommodation requirements in paragraph 47 continue to be met. If the marriage does take place an application for extension of stay on the basis of the marriage is to be considered under paragraph 131.

131. Where a person with limited leave seeks an extension of stay on the basis of marriage to a person settled here, an extension will not be granted unless the Secretary of State is satisfied:

(a)   that the marriage was not entered into primarily to obtain settlement here; and

(b)   that the parties to the marriage have met; and

(c)   that the applicant has not remained in breach of the immigration laws; and

(d)   that the marriage has not taken place after a decision has been made to deport him or he has been recommended for deportation or been given notice under section 6(2) of the Immigration Act 1971; and

(e)   that the marriage has not been terminated; and

(f)   that each of the parties has the intention of living permanently with the other as his or her spouse; and

(g)   that there will be adequate accommodation for the parties and their dependents without recourse to public funds in accommodation of their own or which they occupy themselves; and

(h)   that the parties will be able to maintain themselves and their dependents adequately without recourse to public funds.

When the Secretary of State is satisfied that all the conditions at (a) to (h) above apply, the applicant will be allowed to remain, for 12 months in the first instance.

132. A person who was admitted for a limited period, or given an extension of stay, as the spouse of a person settled here, may have the time limit on their stay removed at the end of that period if the Secretary of State is satisfied that the marriage has not been terminated and that each of the parties has the intention of living permanently with the other as his or her spouse.'

Back in 1987, Stefanie Grant had quite correctly emphasised the fickle history of the rule changes concerning husbands: five changes in 15 years illustrated 'the sensitivity which marriage has acquired as a result of the strict limits placed on primary immigration' (Grant 1987:39). Surely, the issue itself was still sensitive in 1990, but the fact that there appeared to be no longer any officially perceived need to change the rules on the admission of spouses in 1990 indicates one of two things. Either it may simply not have been possible to tighten the screws any further, or there was no real need for revised rules, since the primary purpose rule had already been so remarkably effective since 1983. Newdick (1985:817) provided figures for this, comparing the situation before and after the shifting of the burden of proof:

'Until the coming into effect of the Immigration Rules 1983... the proportion of men from the Indian subcontinent refused entry, either wholly or partly on this ground, was 18 per cent of all refusals and 13 per cent of all decisions to grant and refuse leave to enter... By 1984 the proportion of men refused entry, either wholly or partly, under this rule, had risen to between 80-90 per cent of all refusals and to about 40 per cent of all applications decided.'

For 1990, when sexually non-discriminatory Rules were in full operation, Vincenzi and Marrington (1992:88-89) have recently cited figures of substantial numbers of refusals of entry clearance from the Indian subcontinent. According to Home Office statistics, in that year alone 810 wives and 2,220 husbands were refused. Such figures represent a great deal of misery and do not include cases of people who have been waiting for decisions for many years.

Thus, while Britain could not totally close the door on foreign spouses, the existing control mechanisms, allowing only a fraction of the actual number of applicants to live in the UK with their spouse and, in many cases, child or children, could superficially create an impression of legality and compliance with human rights standards. In practice, as far too many law-abiding citizens know from first-hand experience, the combined effect of strict burden of proof requirements and especially the discretion vested in immigration officers has ensured a most sensitive ongoing fine-tuning process that required no further law-making.

At the same time, as was noted occasionally, but not much discussed initially, the position of EEC spouses was clearly much better than that of UK citizens (see e.g. Sondhi 1987:16), so that English law was again facing a challenge from Europe over discriminatory immigration regulations. Not surprisingly, this situation gave rise to a peculiar strategy by British citizens with primary purpose problems. They would gradually begin to explore settlement in Europe and would then return to Britain under the free movement provisions of EEC law. The recent test case of *Surinder Singh*, to which we referred in the beginning of this study, has shown that this is a viable if circuitous route of entry into Britain. It remains to be seen at the time of writing how the British Immigration Rules will react to this new challenge.

It appears, then, that Nuala Mole was right in her cautiously optimistic conclusion, a few years ago, that at the end of the day, those couples who had the stamina, and were fortunate enough to be given the right kind of advice, would be able to overcome the hurdles of the primary purpose rule. Her wise words deserve to be cited here in full:

> 'The conclusion to be drawn from experience gained in negotiating the maze of regulations regarding the right of husband and wife to live together in the UK can only be this: those couples who are determined that no number of obstacles laid in their way will in the end prevent them from living together in the country of their choice may eventually be allowed to make their matrimonial home in the UK. The faint-hearted and the ill-advised will unfortunately often forfeit their rights along the way. Few will find the journey easy.' (Mole 1987:37).

Chapter 4

The case-law on the primary purpose rule

The previous chapter described in detail how the primary purpose rule was gradually developed to its present sophisticated state by a combination of specific laws, frequent rule changes and secretive but purposeful instructions from the Home Office. In addition to this, typical of a common law system, a body of case-law has built up. It has gradually played a more prominent role in the application of the primary purpose rule.

We have already observed how this process started only in 1984 (see Bhabha et al. 1985:71). After that, the focus of British immigration control with reference to fiancé(e)s and spouses has gradually shifted away from the offices of immigration officials and the Home Office to the judicial arena. This has had the effect of putting the Immigration Appeal Tribunal and increasingly the higher courts into a position from where they could lead and dominate the discussion of the basic as well as the finer points of British immigration control. That the higher courts have become extremely busy with judicial review cases on immigration, which account for up to 25% of their workload, is no secret (see for example the Foreword of Lord Justice Woolf to Cotran et al. 1991). The potentially negative side of this burdensome overload has recently been stressed by Rick Scannell (1992).

The present chapter looks in detail at the development of the case-law on primary purpose. The various techniques of exclusionary practice developed by the British immigration law system and its specific targeting of South Asian spouses will become still more obvious in this context.

The material is again divided into several sections. We begin with a brief sub-chapter on the difficulties of understanding South Asian marriage systems and then return to the issue of marriages of convenience and the difficulties of defining 'primary purpose'. Later sub-chapter first focus on the early case-law on primary purpose, showing how the originally liberal approach by the superior courts could not be maintained. Subsequent developments reveal a vacillation of the higher judiciary between genuine human rights concerns and a thinly veiled desire to come to grips with the 'numbers issue' and the allegations of abuse by immigrants. Judicial review cases, in particular, often have to assess the impact of discretion by immigration officials; here again, there is vacillation between seeking safeguards from arbitrariness and a desire to have a firm system of immigration control for non-white persons. As Mole (see p.105 above) has emphasised, couples wishing to stay together will need considerable stamina, to overcome the many hurdles in their way.

■ 4.1 The ambivalent approach to South Asian marriages

We have already seen that the legislative and administrative efforts to control non-white immigration to Britain have been directed mainly against South Asians. Although primary purpose cases have formed an important part of many immigration lawyers' practice, and there is a long line of reported and unreported cases, it is significant that academic writing on most aspects of the primary purpose rule is still quite underdeveloped. Generally speaking, in Britain, there appears to be a lack of academic interest in immigration law, a subject which is still tacked onto constitutional or administrative law courses, as Ian Macdonald has repeatedly pointed out, if indeed it is taught at all. As a result, neither immigration law itself, nor difficult and contentious subjects like the primary purpose rule have been given as much attention as they deserve.

It also appears that immigration law, as a necessarily multidisciplinary area of work, has put off academic writers. For example, South Asian law and immigration law have only recently been seen as interconnected (see Pearl 1986; Menski 1990). Since very few academics work on South Asian laws anyway, the link with immigration law may be somewhat peripheral and tenuous; similar difficulties arise for African law, other Asian jurisdictions and, as we now experience, Eastern European laws. One might also detect lack of academic interest in a difficult and specialised field of law which has only recently come of age and is, quite properly, dominated by lawyers in practice. In various law colleges, however, there is now clear evidence of a growing demand for courses in immigration law and related subjects and we are likely to see new developments in this area very soon.

Practitioners themselves often explain the scarcity of published material by reference to lack of time to write books and learned articles. No doubt, many immigration lawyers have been kept so busy working on behalf of spouses caught up in the primary purpose rule that there was really no time left to consider the subject in published work. Specialist lawyers would probably not need to read academic articles on primary purpose anyway. Fortunately, some experienced lawyers have considered it important to make their knowledge available to others, so we find a number of articles in *Immigration and Nationality Law and Practice* (for a full index see Ross and Menski 1992; Menski and Bhavsar 1992) and relevant sections in practice handbooks (Mole

1987:25-37; Macdonald 1987:220-237; Macdonald and Blake 1991:260-265; Cotran et al. 1991: Division IV Settlement).

The fact that the primary purpose case-law is so recent has meant that important earlier studies (e.g. Evans 1983; Bhabha et al. 1985; Newdick 1985; Marrington 1985; Bevan 1986, Sondhi 1987) could cover only the early beginnings of the reported case-law, while the bulk of material has only appeared after 1985. Phil Powell has produced a continuously updated volume of *Notes for UK immigration lawyers on custom & practice in the Indian sub-continent* (now Powell 1992) since January 1990, and there have been a few journal articles that focus on the case-law under the primary purpose rule (Rees 1989; now Scannell 1992).

The ambiguous approach taken to applications for settlement in the UK by spouses from South Asia (see in some detail Sondhi 1987:76-78) clearly arises, as we saw in the previous chapter, from white people's fear of being 'swamped', which seems centrally linked with South Asian men. Thus, a report by the Select Committee on Race Relations and Immigration in 1978, calling for controls on the entry rights of fiancées was rejected by the Government on the basis that there was 'little evidence of abuse' by *women* (Bevan 1986:256), which implied that *male* immigration needed to be curtailed. Even today, it is quite apparent that attention is focused on South Asian men, much more than on women from the region (see Macdonald and Blake 1991:260). Among the most recent cases, however, there appears to be a noticeable increase in the number of female spouses facing refusals.

The fact that after the restrictions on primary migration in 1962, during the early 1970s in particular, some South Asian men started to apply for settlement in Britain as the spouses or fiancés of women settled in Britain clearly raised suspicions of ulterior motives; these are still with us today but are now rarely expressed openly. For example, Griffith (1991:181) indicates quite subtly that 'it was recognised that deception took place on a considerable scale', tempting the courts to overreact and to set unduly high standards of proof in some cases. On the other hand, genuine attempts were made in some of the early case-law, as we shall see below, to understand South Asian cultural phenomena and to assess the motives of spouses who applied for entry clearance in the light of such factors.

As Nuala Mole, one of the leading British experts in the field of family settlement, has clearly shown, the early approach of looking at cases 'as a whole' (Mole 1987:29) or 'in the round' would inevitably find a lot of genuine South Asian marriages, parties to which would thus have to be allowed to live together in the UK. In reaction to this, as Griffith (1991:181) would seem to indicate, successive British governments, having decided on a policy of strict immigration control, tightened the immigration rules in disregard of South Asian customs and expected the judges to follow this with less liberal rulings. Scannell (1992:3) emphasises that there was initially quite considerable judicial sympathy for the victims of executive restrictiveness:

'It seemed (in a small way at least) that the judiciary were prepared to add their voice to the widespread and entirely justifiable condemnation and anger felt both by those affected by the operation of the rule and by practitioners trying to overcome its inequities.'

However, as we shall see below in some detail, and as Scannell (1992) has emphasised with reference to the then unreported decision of the Court of Appeal in *Sumeina Masood* (9 July 1991; see now [1992] ImmAR 69]), this judicial sympathy is now in danger of being further eroded by judges who are either unwilling or unable to understand the nature of South Asian marriage arrangements and the implications of their own decisions on the human rights of South Asians and other ethnic minorities in Britain.

Even if it would appear at the moment, after the case of *Surinder Singh*, that recourse to European law may lead to the eventual collapse of the exclusionary mechanism of the primary purpose rule, the underlying ambivalence against the continued immigration of South Asian spouses to Britain and, by implication, to Europe, will not disappear. This adds spice to the topic, but means that many things which have remained unsaid for a long time will not be openly discussed in a climate of fear about worsening community relations and a further increase in Britain's non-white population.

Apart from the more political issues, one particular problem regarding South Asian marriage cases has often been the question of proof of the marriage itself. The Home Office will regularly question the validity of South Asian marriages when the slightest unusual feature is shown (Mole 1987:39). Expert evidence may need to be called for in such cases, since it appears that presenting officers will purposely pick up quaint aspects of South Asian laws, leaving the applicant's lawyer to find an adequate response (see Menski 1990:64).

Apart from the question of performing customary rituals, which in Indian Hindu law remains the dominant criterion (see now *Prasadhkumar* at 1992(1) *Kerala Law Times* 729), some weight may obviously be given to 'direct' evidence that a marriage has taken place. In *Khanom* ([1979-80] Imm AR 182), it was held that it is not essential to pin-point the precise date of a marriage, since the overall question for determination is whether the parties are married. But it was also said that the discovery of a false date will clearly influence the credibility of the statements of applicants and their sponsors. According to Bevan (1986:244), the Home Office does not regard memoranda under the *Hindu Marriage Act*, 1955 of India as sufficient evidence of the existence of the claimed marriage, which shows the official distrust and unhelpful attitude towards anything South Asian. On the other hand, foreign customs and law can be persuasive, for example the fact that cohabitation raises a presumption of marriage under Muslim law (see *Begum* [1978] Imm AR 174; *Channo Bi* [1978] Imm AR 182; *Class-Peter* [1981] Imm AR 154; Macdonald and Blake 1991:249-250). That the same presumption should also be applied under Hindu law seems much less known (but see Desai 1982:748).

A marriage is recognised as valid under English law if the formalities of the place of celebration are complied with and the parties have capacity to marry according to the laws of their domicile (on this see in detail Bromley and Lowe 1987:56-68; Macdonald and Blake 1991: 253-255). Consequences of this could be the recognition of the marriage of young children (*Mohamed* v. *Knott* [1969] 1 QB 1), or the marriage by telephone of a man in England and a woman in Pakistan (Bevan 1986:244). However, English courts retain the power to refuse recognition of foreign law through the use of public policy arguments and appear now more ready to do so if the circumstances of a case are seen as offensive to public morality, or simply not in line with the perceived need 'to protect certain core values in English society' (Poulter 1986:vi). *The Immigration Act*, 1988 and the Immigration Rules, as we saw, have quite clearly tightened up on recognising the effects of South Asian laws when it comes to child marriages and polygamous unions.

The situation has changed quite drastically within a couple of years. Female (but not male) cohabitees still used to be allowed entry under Rule 49 of H.C. 169, which was repealed in August 1985 by HC 503. Entry clearance was granted provided that the relationship with the UK sponsor was a permanent one, the previous marriages of the parties had broken down permanently and no other cohabitees had been admitted already. Evidence of foreign custom would often be crucial to support a particular case.

It has been held that this concession was not intended to facilitate the entry of a harem (*Zahra* [1979-80] Imm AR 48). More recently, as Macdonald and Blake (1991:256-257) explain in some detail, the Rules no longer make provision for the admission of persons who are not legally married, though Home Office instructions allow discretion to be exercised in certain cases.

Phil Powell's work (1992) probably shows most clearly how important detailed recourse to the principles of the various South Asian laws continues to be. There can be no doubt that much more work needs to be done in this field and that, when it comes to judicial decisions on immigration matters involving South Asians, expert guidance on South Asian laws continues to be an important element of the decision-making process.

■ 4.2 Marriages of convenience and primary purpose

As we saw already, the problems of understanding the concept of 'primary purpose', the development of the British primary purpose rule itself and its operation are linked, in a number of ways, with the concept of 'marriage of convenience'. Traditional notions of a marriage of convenience would probably involve marriage arrangements where either spouse found it convenient to be married to the other to obtain certain benefits (on some reported cases see Macdonald and Blake 1991:257). Such benefits would not necessarily be in the form of entry rights to the UK, but our present discussion will obviously focus on this point.

With particular reference to the primary purpose rule, Macdonald stated that the primary purpose rule is different from the marriage of convenience rule and 'in effect it comprises the first half of that rule' (Macdonald 1987:234). This means, as he had stated earlier, that the marriage was primarily entered into to obtain settlement (Macdonald 1987:228). In effect this means that the development of the primary purpose rule depended much more on the above line of argumentation than on the second element of the classical marriage of convenience, namely that there was no real intention to live together permanently as man and wife (Macdonald 1987:228). As we shall see, the early case-law illustrates why this second criterion could not become central to developing the full-blown primary purpose rule: it could not be shown in enough cases that there was no intention of living together permanently (see clearly Mole 1987:28-29). Thus, this approach simply did not lead to enough refusals and could therefore not be continued if the overarching policy aim was a significant reduction in the numbers of male immigrants to the UK from the subcontinent.

The focus of attention thus fell on the motives of applicants in terms of settlement in the UK rather than stability and genuineness of the marriage. Of course, once primary immigration to Britain had been more and more curtailed after the *Commonwealth Immigrants Act* of 1962, marrying a person resident in Britain and seeking admission as a fiancé(e) or spouse became one of the increasingly few avenues of gaining entry to the UK for South Asian men. But how was it possible to ascertain that a particular man really married a British-based woman only to be able to come to Britain? The impossibility of determining the primary purpose of a marriage with any degree of accuracy has been emphasised by Christopher Newdick in an interesting article that appears to have escaped the wide attention it deserves:

> 'Once it is accepted that marriages may be undertaken for a variety of purposes, it is in principle quite legitimate to exclude those who use it as a device for avoiding immigration controls. On the other hand, if the rule is to be used against those whose marriages are acknowledged to be perfectly genuine, care must be taken to avoid using the rule in a way that is harsh and unfair and likely to offend a sense of justice.' (Newdick 1985:816).

The same author commented further that:

'Discovering the nature of a person's motives for behaviour is notoriously difficult. The task of attempting to rank in order of *priority* the purposes for which a marriage has been, or will be, undertaken, serves to add to these complications. If a husband is looking forward to joining his wife, and other members of his family, to regular employment, and to a higher standard of living, how should this variety of aspirations be assessed in terms of their relative importance? And to whose purposes should the entry clearance officer have regard, to those of the man, the woman, or the parents of either or both?' (Newdick 1985:816-817).

The last question posed here, in particular, points us to the important issue again whether British immigration law has ever adequately concerned itself with the legitimate expectations of British-based Asian women.

As Newdick merely indicates, quite subtly, but we know from the community point of view, the standard explanation that South Asian men came to Britain as spouses because they could not come as workers is clearly a one-sided perspective fed by xenophobia. A major reason why South Asian men have continued to come to Britain, often indeed reluctantly, is because their female spouses are settled in Britain and wish to remain here rather than moving to the subcontinent.

By focusing on attempts to identify the 'primary purpose' of male applicants for settlement in Britain, the needs, expectations, and ultimately human rights of British Asian women and their families, it appears, have simply been ignored by the English legal system.

Further, the assumption that many Asians will marry for convenience of immigration flies in the face of statistical and demographic evidence, which is so conveniently unspecific in Britain on many important points. Thus, unless young Asian women who are growing up and are resident and domiciled in Britain were to marry white men (or even, in *Mississippi Masala* style, Afro-Caribbean men) or were to remain unmarried, with whom could they enter married life in Britain if a large number of young Asian men in Britain marry a wife from overseas? There appears to be evidence of a noticeable demographic imbalance here, with new consequences for many young Asian women in Britain. This situation has arisen not only because immigration laws would not raise such a strong presumption of 'marriage of convenience' if the immigrating spouse is female (Mole 1987:26; Macdonald and Blake 1991:260). It is also due to the fact that, simply put, girls from the subcontinent are considered better home makers and less 'spoilt' than girls that grew up in Britain, so are preferred to 'local' Asian girls (see Kannan 1978:137).

But this explanation on its own is far too simple. In reality, largely as a result of British colonial intervention, South Asians have been spread all over the world. Many South Asian families, following the traumas of partition in India/Pakistan in 1947 and the expulsion of Asians from Uganda in 1979, have made a conscious decision not to have all family members (and often business interests) in any one country. The ongoing Fiji crisis has strengthened South Asian people's awareness about their tenuous position as minorities claiming a share in status and power. Occasional veiled threats about repatriation for Asians, whether in Kenya or Britain, keep many people alert to this issue. The relevant consequence for our present discussion is that as a result of family strategies of international dispersal, marriage alliances among Asian families have now often acquired an international dimension and are not singularly directed at Britain. Lack of awareness of this pattern has clearly meant that a few thousand South Asian spouses seeking entry to Britain on the basis of marriage have been publicly declared a serious problem which necessitates legal intervention, while nobody seems able and willing to tell us how many South Asians, male and female, are actually leaving Britain at the same time, and as a result of the same processes of making international marriage arrangements. It is simply too self-flattering to assume, and dishonest to claim, that Britain is top of the list of preferred destinations. The officially nurtured impression of a virtual siege from millions of desperate young men who would use marriage arrangements as a convenient excuse to enter Britain for ever is, thus, questionable on several strong grounds (see also Bevan 1986:253-254).

Without referring in detail to the above points, Newdick elaborated in a significant way on the difficulties of proving that one's client's primary purpose was not that of entry to the UK. Commenting on the Home Office guidelines to immigration officers, his conclusion is quite clear:

> 'In reality, the discovery of the motives that lie behind a person's course of action are vastly more difficult to determine than either the Immigration Rules or the Home Office guidelines indicate. Whilst a marriage of convenience, as a sham, may be identified relatively easily, the bona fide marriage, entered into primarily for immigration purposes, is very difficult to pin-point with any degree of certainty. There are no objective criteria by which a person's motives for action can be arranged in order of priority. The judgement of the entry clearance officer under the primary purpose rule is, therefore, wholly dependent on the *impression* he forms of the facts of the case before him.' (Newdick 1985:817).

This element of subjectivity and official discretion would, obviously, be open to challenge. It is interesting to read today that Newdick, in 1985, emphasised that appeals in cases of this type 'are unlikely to be successful' Newdick (1985:817), though he was by then aware of some of the early unreported cases in which appeals were indeed won. By writing that in view of the uncertainty about motives 'a premium has been placed on the location of the burden of proof' (Newdick 1985:817), the author pin-points precisely the major future hurdle of applications for settlement by male spouses:

> 'There are likely to be cases in which the party who bears the burden will be put to a disadvantage so onerous that he will be unable to establish his case.' (Newdick 1985:817).

The subsequent development of the case-law on primary purpose has indeed confirmed the worst fears of Newdick and many others. In their desperate attempt to exclude South Asians and to keep numbers down, the Home Office and its officials have for many years been making full use of the discretionary powers available to them in determining 'primary purpose' by subjective impression, in other words, by allowing free scope for the misguided assumption that South Asians and other people from Asia and Africa must all be desperate to come to Britain. Newdick himself points out in his conclusions that the issue of numbers, notwithstanding the legitimacy of the principle (see also Bevan 1986:252), is simply a convenient smokescreen for unjust exclusionary mechanisms:

> 'It may be quite proper to exclude those who attempt to use marriage as a device to gain entry to this country, but when that objective is given effect in so crude and insensitive a way as to prejudice those who have legitimate expectations to live here, it is right to call for change.' (Newdick 1985:818).

Immigration statistics clearly show that despite tighter immigration controls, many thousands of people, from the Indian sub-continent in particular, but also from elsewhere in the New Commonwealth, the Old Commonwealth and from Europe, have been coming to Britain for settlement year after year, while Britain is also losing a large number of people every year through emigration. It is apparent that the number of South Asians entering Britain was significantly reduced over time, however. Banton (1988:90) gives a figure of 148,000 entrants from India during 1965-74 and 64,000 during 1975-84, the corresponding figures for Pakistan being 72,000 and 63,000, and for Bangladesh 10,000 and 20,000. This means that many South Asians have continued to come to Britain year after year, too many, it would appear, for the law to take no action.

Since the category of spouses began to form one of the most numerous categories of new applicants for entry to Britain, it is not surprising that efforts at reducing the number of new entrants have focused so clearly on the immigration rules for fiancé(e)s and spouses. While English law could obviously not defend a basic rule that one cannot marry a foreigner who would then seek entry to Britain (on this point see also Bevan 1986:253), strong mechanisms of discouragement or deterrence, including the primary purpose rule, have been developed to achieve precisely that effect.

In that situation, Asian girls in Britain are, it appears, expected to marry men overseas and to stay there with them. This is an implied repatriation policy affecting mainly young women of a particular group; this would appear to be a clear case of indirect institutional discrimination.

If such women argued, as many do, that they have grown up in Britain and want to stay in the place that they know and in which they may have built up their own career, rather than settling in a foreign country, the response of the law is still that the man such a woman chooses to marry will be suspected of marrying her only because he can, in this way, gain entry into Britain (see Macdonald and Blake 1991:263-264; now Scannell 1992). We have already questioned the notion that Britain is necessarily seen as an ideal place to settle down, but where a British Asian woman insists that she wishes to lead her married life in Britain, can we really speak of marriage of convenience or even of primary purpose for the man? Maybe her understanding of convenience and his aspirations symbiotically match, leading to a happy marriage, which may of course still be wrecked by the primary purpose rule. If we follow Rick Scannell in his analysis of recent case-law, couples in the above situation would certainly fall foul of the primary purpose rule if the recent Court of Appeal ruling of Lord Justice Glidewell in *Sumeina Masood* v. *Immigration Appeal Tribunal* ([1992] Imm AR 69) were to be followed. But virtually to insist that British Asian women, because they are women, should settle into married life in South Asia takes adherence to 'tradition' and 'custom' rather too far.

The fact that many South Asians from Britain actually do settle 'back home' and that many women from Britain do get married in India or Pakistan, or now frequently emigrate to other countries to join their husbands there, is far too little known. If we had proper statistical evidence, we would probably find that the movement of Asians across national borders on the occasion of marriage is a movement in all kinds of directions. In other words, the assumption that young Asians will do anything to marry someone in Britain to obtain settlement rights is not based on sound facts at all. It is rather a conveniently floated myth that fits in with notions of 'swamping' and 'floodgates'. It also justifies and legitimises the current British immigration law with its clearly exclusionary policies directed at certain communities.

The facile assumption that Asian marriages are, if not marriages of convenience, then certainly cleverly arranged devices to get round immigration controls, often with little regard for the welfare of the individuals involved in this process, has led to three major tests that intending immigrants have to pass. Macdonald and Blake (1991:260) list them as (i) the primary purpose test, (ii) the intention to live permanently as husband and wife, and (iii) the requirement that the parties have met. On top of this, obviously, there are now increasingly strict maintenance and accommodation requirements to be satisfied (see Gillespie 1992).

The genuineness of a marital relationship may be tested in a variety of ways also after entry clearance has initially been granted. The technique of using probationary periods, as we already noted in the previous chapter, allowed Home Office officials to check up on people's marital relations. Even where initially all required conditions have been fulfilled, only limited leave to enter will be granted anyway. For fiancé(e)s, an extension may be granted if the intended marriage has not taken place within six months, provided good cause is shown for the delay (for details see Macdonald and Blake 1991:259 and 266). Clearly, however, if a marriage does not actually take place, the applicant's claim to remain in Britain will be refused, since the genuineness of the intention to marry will be doubted. Yet this kind of case will be rare, since:

> 'In practice it is far more difficult to satisfy an ECO of both the primary purpose and the genuineness and permanence of a relationship which is still in an inchoate state.' (Mole 1987:26-27).

If, as suggested, fiancés find the initial hurdle higher than husbands, we would encounter cases where the marriage was entered into, marital relations have broken down, the couple has separated and could already be in the process of obtaining a divorce. If either spouse is still subject to temporary leave to remain, this will be fatal to a claim for extension of stay (Macdonald and Blake 1991:266). It appears that in practice such cases have recently gained in prominence, indicating both more frequent breakdown of marriages among Asians in Britain and a tougher attitude by the immigration authorities.

Indeed, there have always been cases where apparently genuine marriages broke down and the spouse with temporary leave to remain (often the wife) faced insurmountable hurdles in extending permission to remain in Britain. Some of these cases have received widespread publicity. Occasionally, especially after local support campaigns, compassionate grounds have been found to extend leave to such a person, while in other cases deportation orders have been implemented.

Such problems would obviously not arise where both spouses have permanent leave to remain, i.e. where the marriage breaks down after a longer time span, even one day after the probation period. Sensible people, it could be said, would ensure that their marriage breaks down only after the immigration restrictions have been removed. In this context, the new stricter rules regarding probationary periods are clearly designed to allow the state to check up on those who might use the classic marriage of convenience avenue to secure entry to Britain. This has created its own problems in the shap of intrusive questioning by officials.

The real problem about 'marriages of convenience', then, is not so much that they occur, but that they are alleged to occur on a wide scale, particularly among Asians. In other words, it is assumed that large numbers of young Asians will only marry a particular spouse because he or she is resident in Britain and would thus give the overseas spouse the right of entry to the UK. This approach assumes, far too simplistically, as we saw, that people would marry someone for a single reason and that marriage as a bond for life can be built on a single aim, such as allowing one spouse to take advantage of the immigration rules in English law that promise entry rights to overseas spouses. This kind of sinister insinuation has, as we saw, been used to legitimise the current system of immigration rules and the strict application of the primary purpose rule, thus denying the obvious fact that Britain's resident Asian population (the same goes, of course, for other ethnic minority communities), with its many links of kinship and allegiance all over the world, may need to create or re-create such links through ties of marriage, visits and other means of keeping and establishing contact in an increasingly international diaspora.

Though the term 'marriage of convenience' is not used in this context any more because we now speak prominently of 'primary purpose', it is obvious that there are some links between the current requirements and the old marriage of convenience rules. If anything, the test has become more difficult, since leave to enter can now be refused to a spouse or intending spouse on grounds of any one of the several requirements under HC 251. In reality applicants are often faced with multiple rejections of their claim to enter the UK for settlement. The strategy underlying multiple rejections is, quite transparently, to avoid mere subjective statements that the deciding officer or judge, as the case may be, did not trust the true purpose of the marriage, as this might give rise to grounds of appeal or other forms of objection to a line of arbitrary decisions. Thus, in practice, and for a variety of reasons, the issue of marriage of convenience has now been relegated to a minor position, while the issue itself is kept alive with allegations of continuous abuse of the marriage rules. The harsh reality for many couples of South Asian origin has therefore been that even parties to a genuine marriage are more than likely to find their application to live together in Britain refused. On this, Macdonald and Blake (1991:265) give rejection rates for 1989 of 63% of all husbands and 73% of all fiancés. The most recent Annual Report of the JCWI (1992:7) emphasises that the Home Office's changed methods of statistical recording now have the deliberately calculated effect of making precise reference to immigration statistics impossible:

> 'It is therefore no longer possible to give precise numbers of couples refused under the primary purpose rule as the results of successful appeals are added to the statistics of those granted entry clearance, even though they will probably have applied in different years.'

The prolonged application of the primary purpose rule as a systematic deterrent strategy has clearly had the long-term effect of ensuring that many South Asian families in Britain will think very carefully now before making marriage arrangements involving a spouse from overseas. The new Home Office policy of exercising discretion in favour of couples after five years of marriage is a further indication that the pressure to desist from international arrangements will not wane. It appears that the strategy of deterrence has been slightly fine-tuned again: rather than claiming, in a subjective manner, that South Asian marriages tend to be 'marriages of convenience' or to rely on 'primary purpose' as a ground for refusal, the new technique amounts probably, as the JCWI argues, to a new quota system:

> 'As the rule is used primarily against applicants from the Indian subcontinent and other South Asian countries, we fear that there will now be an unofficial five-year waiting period for couples in these areas, operating as a disguised quota system to regulate migration.' (JCWI 1992:8).

Though very little has been written about this as yet, the impression is certainly that the primary purpose rule, as a central plank of British immigration control, has also been used as a long-term policy tool to restrain the growth of a South Asian resident population in Britain. Given such obviously discriminatory underlying policy aims, the legal niceties of deciding cases on the primary purpose rule would need to take into account the constant danger of challenge to the rule itself on grounds of unreasonableness or human rights objections, both from within Britain and from the perspective of European law. The vacillation of the British case-law on the primary purpose rule, as we shall see below, between accepting the human dimension of marriage and the inhuman aim of separating couples for the sake of fulfilling more or less hidden immigration policy agenda, will provide an interesting test of judicial perceptiveness about what Bevan (1986:253) called 'a gamut of powerful and well-rehearsed emotions'. Under the primary purpose rule as developed in Britain, can human dignity prevail over ethnic pride and xenophobia?

■ 4.3 The early case-law and its effects

The few studies that were able to comment on the earliest primary purpose cases convey a clear picture of judicial attempts to make sense of South Asian marriage patterns, on the one hand, and to implement the government policy of restrictive immigration control, on the other. Useful coverage of this contentious discourse is found in Mole (1987:28-29), Marrington (1985:539-540), Bhabha et al.(1985:68-72) and Macdonald (1987:233-237), while Sondhi (1987:76-106) provides detailed material describing the dilemmas arising in particular cases and factual situations. Dave Marrington, having given a brief summary of the development of the primary purpose rule (Marrington 1985:536-539), proceeds to consider how the Immigration Appeal Tribunal (IAT) dealt with the early cases.

Thus, in the unreported case of *Naresh Kumar* (3278), a determination notified on 21st June 1984, it was found that the appellant husband had married a British citizen soon after obtaining leave to enter as a visitor. When he applied for leave to remain in Britain on the basis of his marriage, he was refused by an adjudicator, it appears, because there was a suspicion that the marriage had been entered into primarily to obtain settlement in Britain. Since there was no dispute about any of the other conditions and it had also been accepted that the marriage was genuine and that the parties intended to live permanently as husband and wife, the only point to determine on appeal was whether the marriage had been entered into *primarily* to obtain settlement. The Immigration Appeal Tribunal clearly stated that, where the couple had established the genuine nature of their marriage on the balance of probabilities, the burden of proof shifted to the Secretary of State to establish that the marriage was entered into primarily to obtain settlement (see also Mole 1987:29).

Marrington (1985:540) emphasises firstly that this approach was at odds with officially stated policy. It contradicted the statements of Home Office officials in Parliament in 1979, when it had been promised that the intentions of the parties would be irrelevant. Secondly, he notes that the IAT had acknowledged explicitly that the fundamental purpose of the institution of marriage was to enable the spouses to live together permanently as husband and wife.

Thus, since the couple in this case had established that they intended to live together permanently, and although the IAT recognised that settlement was a factor in this case, Naresh Kumar saw his appeal allowed.

This decision was then applied in a number of other unreported cases, *Surinder* (3128), *Ravinder Singh* (3352) and *Lambhikar Singh* (3353), referred to by Marrington (1985:540) and Bhabha et al.(1985:71) as *Lahmber Singh*. Notably, all these cases involved Panjabi men, i.e. males from communities that had been prominent as primary migrants prior to the *Commonwealth Immigrants Act,* 1962 and that had now established firm roots in Britain, leading to intercontinental marriages. These men stated quite clearly that they had various reasons to come to the UK other than marriage, be they the presence of close relatives, as in *Ravinder Singh* (Bhabha et al. 1985:71) or economic motives, as expressed in *Lambhikar Singh* (Bhabha et al. 1985:71).

In all these cases, the IAT saw the intention of the parties to live together permanently, rather than settlement in the UK, as the 'primary purpose' of the marriage and thus allowed the appeals. On the basis of such evidence, Nuala Mole has suggested that in this early stage of case-law, members of the IAT were genuinely attempting to understand the situation of the spouses rather than actively seeking to implement government policy in terms of exercising strict immigration control:

> 'Where there was clearly a genuine and permanent relationship the earliest determinations of the appellate authorities often took the approach that when the evidence was looked at as a whole it was unlikely that the marriage had been entered into 'primarily' to obtain settlement. This was held to be so even where 'the obtaining of settlement in the UK was an important factor in the minds of everyone' (Surinder (3128)).' (Mole 1987:29).

In *Ravinder Singh* (3352) and *Lambhikar Singh* (3353), the IAT went further and acknowledged explicitly that, even where it was obvious that one purpose of the marriage was admission of the appellant to the UK, this did not rebut the *prima facie* evidence of a South Asian arranged marriage which had been entered into with the primary purpose that the parties should live together permanently. It appears that especially in *Ravinder Singh* (3352), the Tribunal showed its awareness of the family context of Asian marriage arrangements and extended its argument, holding that:

> '...one purpose of the arranged marriage was clearly to obtain the appellant's admission to the UK. On the evidence such a purpose cannot be said in its family context to displace the usual primary purpose of marriage as we know it — the intention to live together.' (cited by Mole 1987:29).

Thus, where the appellant's admission to the UK was clearly one purpose of the marriage, this did not automatically mean that there was no intention of the spouses to live together, and the notion of 'marriage of convenience' could not be applied to exclude the applicant. These early decisions, which one could see as commonsensical attempts to understand the psychology of Asian marriage arrangements, clearly took notice of the multiplicity of factors that influence the decision to marry a particular person, who will then apply for entry clearance. The contrast with the recent judgement by Glidewell LJ in *Sumeina Masood* ([1992] ImmAR 69; see Scannell 1992) is remarkable.

Macdonald (1987:233-234) has looked at the same cases more from the perspective of the practising lawyer and has emphasised the important role of the burden of proof in this discussion. He distinguishes the primary purpose rule from the marriage of convenience rule and shows how, in the early cases referred to above, admission to the UK could only be refused if both requirements of the marriage rules were not fulfilled. The early cases are, thus, very significant for the discussion of the relationship between the various limbs of the primary purpose rule.

Macdonald (1987:234) thus brings out clearly that *Ravinder Singh* (3352) and *Lambhikar Singh* (3353) extended the proposition that once the applicant had shown that part (b) of the rule, intention to live together permanently as husband and wife, had been proved, this would satisfy element (a) also, unless the immigration authorities proved otherwise.

The results of these cases, in terms of immigration control, must have caused alarm among those opposed to any further immigration. The system of immigration controls for spouses, as introduced in February 1983, when HC 169 came into operation, was clearly not an effective means of keeping down the number of South Asian men seeking to enter Britain. Marrington (1985:540) tells us that:

'By mid-1984 it seemed that the objective of the immigration rules draftsmen — to divorce the intentions of the parties from the purpose of the marriage — had failed. The unwillingness of the tribunal to devalue the arranged marriage, and its insistence that the presumptive primary purpose of the institution was permanent cohabitation, evidenced an inter-cultural tolerance which was perhaps inconsistent with the aims of the executive and against the current of immigration control.'

Macdonald and Blake (1991:260-261), too, comment on this early dilemma created by *Naresh Kumar* (3278) and the cases that followed it. If the implication of these early decisions was that once intention to live together permanently had been proved, this would more or less automatically negate the argument that the marriage had been entered into primarily to gain settlement in the UK. Now reasonableness had to give way to discretionary powers and arbitrariness if one wanted to curtail the numbers of potential applicants by deterrence and, more urgently, if the aim was to reduce the chances of successful appeals against refusals for entry clearance as spouses.

This dilemma of the early 1980s, focusing on the burden of proof, helps us to understand why we can today see innumerable perfectly genuine marriages among South Asians, with spouses who have been married for years, have children and are obviously not parties to sham arrangements for the purpose of immigration — but who are still divided by British immigration law. Obviously, between the early commonsense approach of 1984 and today, there is a vast difference in how the applications of Asian spouses for settlement in the UK are dealt with. The fine-tuned restrictive approach, as we shall see shortly, is clearly not genuinely interested in assessing the true and real purpose of South Asian marriage arrangements, but is constrained and overshadowed by instructions to keep the numbers of new immigrants down to acceptable levels. Thus, no matter how many people apply for entry clearance or settlement on the ground of marriage or engagement, and no matter how genuine the marriage may be, the main purpose of the legal machinery, it appears, is no longer to assess and decide the claims of the applicants or, more likely, appellants, but to implement a policy decision not to let in more than a certain number of people per year.

■ 4.4 Tightening the screws: *Vinod Bhatia*

Bhabha et al. (1985:69-71) analyse clearly how the dilemma arising from the liberal mid-1984 IAT decisions was tackled. Rather than directly prevailing upon the IAT to change its policy, secret instructions were issued to entry clearance officers to develop intrusive practices of interrogation that would provide more evidence of the 'primary purpose' of male applicants (see also Newdick 1985:817). Since the early IAT decisions were to the effect that the onus of proof might come to rest on the Secretary of State to show that a marriage was primarily entered into to obtain settlement, the scope for discretion of the entry clearance officers needed to be exploited more fully. In particular, as Bhabha et al. (1985:70) emphasise, the secret instructions concluded that at the end of the interrogation the applicant,

> "should *not* be given the benefit of the doubt'.... if the evidence is evenly balanced, for in that case he has not been able to *prove* that the marriage was not primarily for immigration purposes.'

This approach must have led to many more initial refusals, with more cases coming up for appeal. But how could one prove what was the main motive or 'primary purpose' for getting married? We noted how Christopher Newdick (1985) warned of the virtual impossibility of solving this conundrum. Similarly, Bhabha et al. (1985:70-71) elaborate on this point. The most effective strategy, though, was to ensure that the case-law would go the way the Home Office wanted.

A two-pronged attack on the IAT decisions of mid-1984 was thus necessary. On the one hand, the immigration officers, armed with their new instructions, would continue to refuse applicants, and would in fact increase their refusal rates, by looking more specifically for evidence of 'primary purpose', thus seeking to devalue evidence that showed the genuineness of South Asian marriages as permanent and stable arrangements. But this, by itself, was not going to change the earlier IAT rulings, so that a new test case was needed to establish a position that would be more favourable towards the aims of immigration control. Thus, the second line of attack was to work towards a re-interpretation of the burden of proof under the existing Immigration Rules. As Macdonald (1987:234) indicates, HC 169 of February 1983 had already switched the burden of proof to the appellant (see also Macdonald and Blake

1991:260). Since the early IAT decisions allowed that burden to be discharged too easily, the case-law would need to develop a new approach.

In the important case of *Vinod Bhatia*, the concept of 'primary purpose' came of age (Marrington 1985:243) and the new aggressive approach to South Asian marriages comes out most clearly in the discussions over this case. In view of the earlier, liberal interpretations of the requirements that had to be fulfilled by men seeking admission to the UK as fiancés or spouses, this case became an important landmark decision, which caused a lot of distress and anguish in the South Asian communities, but also led to greater co-operation between human rights lawyers and the growing number of immigration experts.

The Tribunal decision in *Vinod Bhatia* is unreported (3456). It was held, by a majority, that the earlier line of authorities was wrong. Since the case ultimately went up to the Court of Appeal, this decision set the scene for the first major courtroom battle over primary purpose in British immigration law.

The case was later heard by the Queen's Bench Division (*Vinod Bhatia* [1985] Imm AR 39) and finally went to the Court of Appeal. *Vinod Bhatia* v. *Immigration Appeal Tribunal* ([1985] Imm AR 50 [CA]) was an important test case on the criteria to be met by male applicants, subject to immigration control under the *Immigration Act*, 1971 and the Rules made thereunder, who sought to enter the United Kingdom for settlement as fiancés of women who were British citizens settled in the UK. The case also decided, in principle, the rules regarding husbands. Approximately 200 cases, at the time, were awaiting the outcome in *Bhatia*, illustrating the point made earlier that the new restrictive policy had led to many refusals. This important case has been discussed in virtually all textbooks on immigration law in some detail (see for example Macdonald 1987:234-235; Mole 1987:29-31; Macdonald and Blake 1991:261; also Pearl 1986:24-25; Griffith 1991:181-183). Though the position established in *Bhatia* was subsequently dissented from in certain respects, this case is important 'in order to appreciate the understanding of the law that would have guided the minds of ECOs and the Home Office throughout the period 1984-86' (Mole 1987:30) and, one can say now, far beyond.

Before we come to the facts of the case, it is perhaps useful to have the relevant paragraph of the Rules in sight. For the sake of brevity, only the relevant requirements of Rule 41 of the Immigration Rules, 1983 (H.C. 169) which applied to this case, are listed here. They were as follows:

(a) that it is not the primary purpose of the intended marriage to obtain admission to the United Kingdom; and

(b) that there is an intention that the parties to the marriage should live together permanently as man and wife; and

(c) that the parties to the proposed marriage have met.

The appellant Vinod Bhatia, a citizen of India, applied for entry clearance as a fiancé in New Delhi in February 1981 to enable him to come to the UK to marry and settle with Vijay Kumari, a woman settled in Britain since 1970, who was a divorcee with a young daughter. This case, therefore, also raised the question of remarriage of Hindu women after divorce and the question of dowries in such situations. As is pointed out in the case itself, it is difficult, if not rare, for an Indian Hindu woman who is divorced to find another husband, a proposition agreed to by Pearl (1986:24), but probably less clear-cut in reality. Vijay Kumari's parents, after looking unsuccessfully for a husband in Britain, placed a matrimonial advert for a suitable husband in the *Hindustan Times* in India.

Bhatia applied and was selected, probably after the kind of process resembling a job interview, as described by Nuala Mole (1987:28). The woman's parents then made the necessary arrangements for the marriage, which was to take place in India.

Entry clearance was subsequently applied for and Bhatia was interviewed in New Delhi, while Vijay Kumari was questioned by an immigration officer in England. Both gave full information about their families and how the marriage had been arranged. The applicant, however, said that he did not think his father would have agreed to the marriage had the woman not been settled in the UK. She stated she was not prepared to live in India because of the education of her daughter. On 17th March 1983, the entry clearance officer in New Delhi refused to grant entry clearance to the husband on the ground that he was not satisfied that it was not the primary purpose of the intended marriage to obtain admission to the UK.

Bhatia's appeal against that decision to an adjudicator was dismissed on 23 March 1984. Bhabha et al. (1985:71) seem to suggest that the Home Office decided to arrange a special tribunal, made up of three professional lawyers. This Tribunal sat on 31st August 1984 and delivered its decision on 1st October 1984. The delay itself is probably significant.

Two out of the three members agreed with the Home Office view that, while the primary purpose of the wife and her family was to arrange a suitable marriage for the woman, the primary purpose of the appellant was to obtain admission to Britain. Thus, in view of the statements made by both spouses, merely discharging the burden of proof as to the intention of the parties to live together permanently was not sufficient to shift the burden, as the earlier cases had held, to the immigration officials in relation to the primary purpose clause. The third member of the tribunal, however, Professor Jackson, stuck to the position established in earlier cases, argued for retaining a general interpretation of 'marriage' and and also brought in concerns about the UK's compliance with EEC law (see Marrington 1985:541). On the basis of the facts before him, he found that,

> '...the evidence comes nowhere near displacing the intention to live together permanently as the primary purpose of this intended marriage.' (cited by Bhabha et al.1985:71).

Vinod Bhatia (3456) was refused admission to the UK by a majority of two to one. The implications were far-reaching and led several authors to comment on the near impossibility of advising clients. While David Pearl (1986:25) wrote that 'it is difficult to advise on the circumstances where an application would succeed', Bhabha et al. (1985:72) noted at the time:

> 'The majority decision means that the Home Office can now continue to refuse almost any man applying to come here to join his wife. Hundreds of British women, including those born here, have already been affected by the application of the 'primary purpose' rule.'

Having held that the burden of proof fell on the applicant, to assist future determination, the Tribunal also established a sliding scale for the discharging of this burden of proof (see Mole (1987:30):

> '(1) At one end of the scale, for example, there are cases in which the applicant has previously made repeated and unsuccessful attempts to gain admission or to settle in this country on various grounds or in which a decision has been made to deport him (in this last instance, the present rules require such an application to be refused, but the earlier rules did not). In such cases the onus upon the appellant must be formidable.
>
> (2) Further down the scale one has cases arranged by a marriage broker or as a result of an advertisement, in which the parties have only met once, possibly simply to satisfy one of the requirements of the rule, and have no previous mutual connections of any kind. In such cases the onus upon the appellant will probably be less formidable, but still considerable.
>
> (3) At the other end of the scale there may be cases in which the families of the proposed bride and groom have known each other a long time, possibly even before coming to this country and there has been a history of inter-marriage between them, a not uncommon practice in India. In such cases the onus upon the appellant will probably be fairly easily discharged.'

While it was recognised that all cases depended on their own peculiar facts (Macdonald 1987:234; Macdonald and Blake 1991:261), the importance of this 'sliding scale' is that the resulting categories, with their attendant qualifications of 'formidable', 'considerable' and 'fairly easily discharged' were thereafter adhered to very rigidly by entry clearance officers, the Home Office and adjudicators alike (Mole 1987:30).

On 3rd April 1985, in *R.* v. *Immigration Appeal Tribunal ex parte Vinod Bhatia* ([1985] ImmAR 39 [QBD]), Mr. Justice Forbes refused an application for judicial review of the decision by the Tribunal. The court confirmed that the burden lies on the applicant, and that there could be no shift of the onus of proof (see Marrington 1985:542). The fiancé or husband had to prove separately that (a) the marriage is genuine and (b) its primary purpose is not settlement in the UK. Criterion (a) need not be conclusive of (b), and an entry clearance officer was not tied to the purposes as expressed by the parties, but could look further afield (Bevan 1986:250; Marrington 1985:542). In this context, it proved extremely helpful for many years to come that entry clearance officers were under instructions to use any available techniques to trap applicants, as illustrated by Bevan (1986:250-251). Thus, not only the motives of the applicant or the parties to the marriage became relevant, but also any evidence about the expectations of the parents of the couple, and any other evidence that the entry clearance officer might find. Thus:

> 'An arranged marriage might well be a genuine marriage in the sense that the parties intended to live together, but the primary purpose of the arrangement (by the parents) might still be to secure admission to the UK.' (Per Forbes J.; quoted at Bevan 1986:250).

The judge in this case went much further in his negative approach by attacking South Asian arranged marriages (see Marrington 1985:542) and by virtually stereotyping South Asian marriages involving a British spouse as immigration marriages. This caused much offence and distress and was criticised by several writers at the time, including Ian Macdonald:

> 'In the Divisional Court Forbes J suggested that entry clearance officers should approach their task of assessing the primary purpose of a marriage against the background of their knowledge of Hindu customs and should take into account the fact that many marriages in the subcontinent had admission to the UK as their primary purpose, and so their proper approach should be one of cautious pessimism.' (Macdonald 1987:234).

The apparent clampdown on South Asian spouses, involving a test that was proudly presented as 'perfectly easy to apply' (see Bevan 1986:250), clearly involved a negative basic attitude to applicants and their case. Thus Mr. Justice Forbes stated:

> 'If there is no clear evidence either way....or if the question.....seems evenly balanced, [the applicant] should no longer be given the benefit of the doubt.' (cited at Bevan 1986:250).

The new situation regarding the burden of proof and the relevance of related evidence created a fresh hurdle for practitioners seeking to bring appeals. As Nuala Mole (1987:31) observed:

> 'Since the question of primary purpose is one of fact, it was difficult to obtain the Tribunal's leave to appeal to them and even more difficult to get leave to have the adjudicator's decisions judicially reviewed.'

In an attempt to reverse the new restrictions imposed by the decision of Mr. Justice Forbes, Mr. Bhatia approached the Court of Appeal. The case is reported as *Vinod Bhatia* v. *Immigration Appeal Tribunal* ([1985] ImmAR 50 [CA]). The Court of Appeal, however, was unsympathetic, specifically mentioned that 'it is rare for an Indian Hindu woman who is divorced to find another husband' (p.51), and then addressed the issue of 'whose purpose'. O'Connor LJ decided that para 41 of HC 169, 'presumes that it is the primary purpose of the intended marriage to obtain admission of the applicant to the United Kingdom.' (p.52).

Thus, even though the comments by Forbes J about an attitude of 'cautious pessimism' were seen by the Court of Appeal as containing pejorative overtones (Macdonald 1987:234), Lord Justice O'Connor here provided an even more anti-immigrant interpretation by deriving a presumption of primary purpose from the Immigration Rules themselves, i.e. from the anti-immigration stance of British legislators. This is clear evidence of a tightening of the assessment of South Asian marriages and of an extremely unsympathetic approach. We shall see below how, a few years later, the position established by the Court of Appeal was seen as going rather too far, but by then the damage had been done: the primary purpose rule was put firmly in place by the test case of *Bhatia*.

The Court of Appeal also did not move away from the position that the applicant alone would have to prove that settlement was not the primary purpose of the marriage. Putting the onus of proof, on the balance of probabilities, firmly on the applicant, the Court of Appeal, like the Divisional Court, refused to entertain any philosophical consideration of the purpose of marriage and thus rejected the argument that a genuine marriage could be *ipso facto* evidence of the absence of the primary purpose of immigration to the UK.

■ 4.5 The post-Bhatia conundrum

The feelings of despair about the Court of Appeal's approach to South Asian marriages in Bhatia's case were certainly shared by Mr. Bhatia himself, who decided that he had had enough and married another woman. As Nuala Mole (1987:31) tells us, it was just as his case was due to be heard by the House of Lords that Mr. Bhatia, 'doubtless wearying of waiting six years already to marry the girl of his choice, married another and the saga came to an end.'

Following *Bhatia*, there was considerable confusion and insecurity among immigration lawyers and their clients about the situational contexts in which a primary purpose appeal from India or Pakistan might be successful. It was also not at all clear after *Bhatia* whose motives were or were not to be taken account of in assessing 'primary purpose'. One effect was certain: there was increasing evidence of higher refusal rates. Thus, by 1985, 48 per cent of all husband and fiancé applications from the subcontinent were refused. Of these, 88% were on the grounds of primary purpose (Mole 1987:31).

During 1985, a number of Tribunal decisions made it somewhat clearer what an applicant's prospects of success were, and also what information the immigration authorities would be likely to call upon. Such cases remained unreported and include *D. Patel* (4373) and *Narinder Singh Sandu* (4352), both referred to below; *Hayat* (4651); *Farouq* (4505) and *Sopariwala* (4318).

The case of *Sopariwala* v. *ECO, Bombay* (4318) was discussed in some detail by Pearl (1986:25-26). The case is interesting because of its circumstances and the fact that the applicant was successful before the IAT. The appellant was a Muslim man from India who had applied for entry clearance to come to the UK to marry and settle with his fiancée, a first cousin. This fact, among many Muslim communities, can be taken as helpful evidence of traditional family arrangements and was, as Pearl (1986:26) indicates, probably the crucial factor that tipped the scales in favour of allowing the appeal.

Complications arose in this case, and led very probably to the original refusal, because the young lady had been married before to another Muslim man. This first marriage had been registered in England, but no religious ceremony had ever taken place and the first husband had later obtained a decree of nullity. As no Muslim ceremony had occurred, the Tribunal was advised that the family did not even consider the woman to have been married; this was accepted practice in the Muslim community. The Tribunal also agreed that the girl's parents must be glad that they had found a suitable husband after the disaster of the first marriage. There was no doubt that the girl's parents wanted the applicant to come and live in the UK. However, the Tribunal was mainly concerned with the applicant's purpose, and found on a balance of probabilities that admission to the UK was not the primary purpose of his application.

Pearl (1986:26) comments that this was very much a borderline case and that an analysis of the cases decided after *Bhatia* by the IAT suggests extremely low chances of winning a similar appeal. On the other hand, Pearl (1986:26) mentions two other successful appeals that were won on the basis of particular facts. In *Narinder Singh Sandu* v. *ECO, Bombay* (4352), an unreported case of 1985, the appellant had a good job in India and was prepared to give it up. In the unreported 1985 case of *Devesh Dhirubhai Patel* v. *ECO, Bombay* (4373), it was a 'love marriage' rather than a traditional arranged marriage. While Pearl warns that 'love marriages' may still be hit by the primary purpose rule, there have certainly been a number of successful applications. Phil Powell's research (1991 and 1992: sheet 4) confirms, however, that pleading 'love' may, in certain circumstances, lead to outright rejection.

In the post-*Bhatia* phase, many more South Asian spouses experienced the anguish and suffering arising from the full-blown development of the primary purpose rule and comparatively few applicants benefited from discretion in their favour. While this rule was partly justified by rhetorical references to good race relations (see Marrington 1985:543), in reality its exclusionary purpose was quite clear and much less conducive to the maintenance of harmonious South Asian family life in Britain than claimed. Keeping out as many young South Asian men as possible and thereby, increasingly, deterring the families of South Asian women in Britain, and the women themselves, from entering any marriage arrangements with men from the subcontinent, became clearly a major focal aim of British immigration control.

Pearl (1986:26-27) has commented in some detail on the two major motives of those who support the primary purpose rule. He found that:

> 'First, the rules are justified as being necessary to provide effective immigra-
> tion control and prevent disguised primary immigration. Secondly, the rules
> are sometimes justified on the basis that they provide protection for girls who
> might be pushed into an unwanted marriage solely to enable a male country-
> man to gain entry to this country.' (Pearl 1986:26).

It would seem that evidence of some cases of 'reluctant brides' has always been eagerly used to demonstrate continuing abuse of the fiancé and husband rules by South Asians during the 1980s. Pearl's discussion (1986:26-27) provides several examples of this problem. He also reports in some detail on the case of *R.* v. *Immigration Appeal Tribunal ex parte Mohammad Bashir* ([1984] ImmAR 165), which focused attention on the related legal problem of marriages broken down during the probationary period. Other writers, notably Bhabha et al. (1985) have emphasised the negative effects that the new exclusionary practices had on South Asian women, in particular, though nobody has, to date, produced a detailed study on this aspect.

At the end of the day, no matter how genuine a particular marriage might be, the couple's marital life could still be ruined by the subjective statement that an immigration official had not been satisfied that it was not the primary purpose of the marriage to obtain settlement rights in the UK for the man. The courts, as we have begun to see would, after 1984, very probably not rescue an applicant from the subjective discretion of entry clearance officers and adjudicators. The fact that such negative decisions were reached only regarding South Asian men has, of course, been widely noted (see for example Macdonald and Blake 1991:260; Macdonald 1987:233-234). A finding of direct or indirect discrimination, however, has skilfully been pre-empted, since para 2 of HC 169 in the 1980s, as well as para 6 under the current Immigration Rules (HC 251) state categorically that:

> 'Immigration officers will carry out their duties without regard to the race, colour or religion of people seeking to enter the United Kingdom.'

The fact that this paragraph in the Immigration Rules has remained unamended would appear to show considerable official confidence in the power of such statements *per se*. The knowledge that early judicial scrutiny of this paragraph, as indicated at p.56 in the judgement of O'Connor LJ in *Vinod Bhatia* v. *Immigration Appeal Tribunal* ([1985] ImmAR 50 [CA]; see also Marrington 1985:543) fortified the impression of non-discriminatory treatment, will have been a source of comfort for those opposed to any relaxation of immigration controls. In technically legal terms, as Vincenzi and Marrington (1992:9-10) have very recently confirmed, this paragraph seems quite unassailable.

However, for many lawyers, advisers, activists and the affected groups of people themselves, i.e. those who have reason to be more sensitive to the possibility of injustice committed in the name of the law, the post-Bhatia phase remained one of considerable frustration and dissatisfaction.

Neither changes in the Immigration Rules, nor more helpful judicial dicta could be expected for some time to come.

■ 4.6 Intervening devotion: a fresh attempt to make sense of 'primary purpose'

A modicum of clarification was achieved by the decision in *R.* v. *Immigration Appeal Tribunal, ex parte Arun Kumar* ([1986] ImmAR 446 [CA]), which came just in time for the second edition of Macdonald's text (1987:235). This decision provided, within limits, a helpful judicial restatement of how entry clearance officers were to determine the thorny question of 'primary purpose'. The technique to clarify this point involved a closer look by the higher courts at the relationship of the spouses after marriage, in effect while they were separated by an earlier rejection of the man's claim. The term coined here, 'intervening devotion', seemed helpful at first sight, but it also led to more intrusive questioning by immigration officials and adjudicators and opened up yet more scope for the refusal to accept traditional South Asian views on marriage and married life. On balance, this case was a mixed blessing, though it appeared less illiberal than *Bhatia*.

The facts of the case were not really unusual. A Hindu Brahmin man from the Panjab in India and a British-born Panjabi Brahmin girl got engaged in 1981. On 25th March 1982, the man, Arun Kumar, sought entry clearance as the fiancé of Santosh Kumari, who duly provided two sponsorship declarations. However, before the fiancé application could be considered, the woman travelled to India where the parties were married on 12th December 1982. She later said that this decision was taken to allow more family members to take part in the wedding, but it was also admitted by the woman that the move to India was designed to avoid further delays to the marriage and the entry clearance application.

After the marriage the parties lived together in India. The man subsequently applied for entry clearance as a husband. Both spouses were interviewed in New Delhi on 21st April 1983. On 8th February 1984, the husband was again interviewed in New Delhi. This time his application was refused, because the ECO was not satisfied that the primary purpose of the marriage was not for the appellant to secure settlement in the UK.

Meanwhile, the wife had returned to the UK in January 1984, for health reasons and because she was pregnant. She suffered a miscarriage a few weeks later, three days after her husband's application had been refused. Then, in January 1985, the wife returned to India for six weeks, but she had to return to Birmingham to attend the husband's appeal before an adjudicator. On 25th March 1985, the husband's appeal was dismissed by the adjudicator. Leave to appeal to the IAT was refused on 26th June 1985, as was an application for judicial review, but a renewed application to the Court of Appeal was granted on 10th February 1986.

While the wife was in India, she had become pregnant again. Probably on compassionate grounds, the husband was admitted to the UK as a visitor on 25th August 1985, and a child was born to them in October 1985. The wife subsequently suffered a further miscarriage.

It should be noted that it took four years to determine an eventual outcome in this case, though this is by no means an unusually long time. In considering the husband's application, the Court of Appeal turned to paragraph 54 of H.C. 169 of 1983 as the relevant set of Immigration Rules in force when the case arose. Lord Justice Nourse, who had also been part of the Court of Appeal in *Bhatia*, delivered the leading judgement, which was followed by a separate judgement by Sir John Donaldson, then Master of the Rolls.

First of all, Nourse LJ was concerned to correct the statement made by the Court of Appeal in *Bhatia*, with which he had concurred then, that the Immigration Rules presumed that it was the primary purpose of the intended marriage to obtain admission of the applicant to the UK. At p. 450 of the judgement we read:

'It is perhaps a little misleading to say that the rule 'presumes' that it is the primary purpose of the intended marriage to obtain admission of the applicant to the United Kingdom. All that it does is to place him under the burden of satisfying the entry clearance officer on the balance of probabilities that that and the other requirements of the rule are duly satisfied.'

In other words, the Court of Appeal was here cautiously retreating from the position that all South Asian marriages involving the entry of the man to Britain were, in essence, to be seen as immigration marriages rather than normal marriages.

The Court of Appeal then found that there was no substantial difference between Rule 41 of HC 169 for fiancés and Rule 54 for husbands, save that under Rule 54(a) an entry clearance officer is obliged to look back at circumstances obtaining when the marriage was entered into, while under Rule 41(a) the assessment of the purpose of the proposed marriage is a matter which relates more particularly to the time of the application under consideration.

It followed from the above finding, however, that events following the marriage may, on a husband application, be material to the evaluation of the purpose of the marriage. In this particular case of a long-suffering divided family, the proved devotion of the couples was a material fact. This part of the judgement gave rise to a phrase which was used to describe the evidenced relationship of the parties whilst the application procedure continued. Evidence of 'the proved devotion' (p.453) between the applicant and the sponsor wife, or 'intervening devotion', as it came to be commonly called, might make it easier to satisfy an ECO or adjudicator that the parties' purpose at the time of the marriage was not primarily to obtain entry to the UK.

It appears, thus, that the undoubted suffering of Arun Kumar and his wife, which had not in the least concerned the adjudicator, who had taken a rather jaundiced view of the Indian arranged marriage system, had some effect on the judges in the Court of Appeal, who found that they could not quite accept the adjudicator's hostile approach to South Asian arranged marriages.

An interesting development in this case was, further, a modified view of the relationship between the requirements in paragraphs 41(a) and 54(a) and in 41(b) and 54(b). This was developed by the Master of the Rolls, who held that though they constituted separate and different requirements, 'evidence bearing on one question will often cast a flood of light on the other.'(p.455).

The Court also confirmed in *Arun Kumar* that in the assessment of the primary purpose of the marriage, the motives of all the persons concerned may be taken into account. However,

> '...an engagement or marriage which is so far removed from the English concept of engagement and marriage that the parties have not even met at the time of application provides no basis for an application for entry clearance.'(p.454).

While he was thus dismissive of marriage arrangements in which the spouses had not even met, Sir John Donaldson, Master of the Rolls, most probably in view of the long-suffering couple in this case, further and crucially held that,

> 'It is only if..... the matrimonial relationship was or may have been of subsidiary importance that the entry clearance officer will fail to be satisfied that it was not an 'immigration' marriage.' (p.455-456).

He therefore recommended that, on the whole, the proper approach should be as a jury might approach a decision, and the ECO should ask himself the question:

'What is or was the real, the primary, the basic object of the exercise in this couple agreeing to get or getting married? Was it to live together as man and wife, preferably in the United Kingdom, or was it to enable the fiancé or husband to obtain entry to the United Kingdom, the matrimonial relationship being of subsidiary importance?' (p.455).

Nuala Mole (1987:32) tells us that practitioners treated this commonsense approach with some relief and comments that:

'It finally seemed that it was at least going to be easier to ascertain what it was couples had to prove, even if genuine marriages would still be struck down for failing to prove it.'

A few years later, however, Macdonald and Blake (1991:262) tell us that the humanitarian spirit of the judgement was largely ignored by the ECOs and some adjudicators. This seems not untypical, as there is considerable evidence, including the case of *Arun Kumar* itself, of extremely hostile attitudes to the South Asian arranged marriage system and its immigration implications for Britain. Thus, it appears from page 455 of the judgement that the adjudicator in Birmingham who refused the appeal of *Arun Kumar* appears to have stated, fully aware of his discretionary powers, that:

'...under the rules a marriage primarily entered into in order to obtain admission to the United Kingdom would still retain its non-qualifying character whatever happened afterwards and even if the husband applied for entry on their Golden Wedding Day.'

The fact that the Master of the Rolls appeared to agree with such a statement did not go unnoticed and must have added to the ambivalence with which *Arun Kumar* has subsequently been viewed. As Macdonald and Blake (1991:261) have pointed out, the Court of Appeal's decision in *Arun Kumar* 'gave considerable assistance to couples who could demonstrate actual cohabitation or proved devotion', but this by no means implied that any genuine South Asian marriage, even after long cohabitation and clear evidence of 'intervening devotion', would lead to happy married life together in the United Kingdom.

■ 4.7 Post-Arun Kumar realism

In an attempt to restate and summarise the position after the Court of Appeal had quashed the decision of the IAT in *Arun Kumar* ([1986] ImmAR 446 [CA]), Ian Macdonald (1987:235-236) provided a list of what he called 'observations'. These eight points are no longer included in the third edition of Macdonald's text, probably because they have been superseded by the famous ten propositions in the case of *Hoque and Singh* ([1988 ImmAR 216), which is discussed in chapter 4.8 below. In brief, Macdonald's observations were as follows:

(i)   The burden of satisfying the immigration authorities that the primary purpose of the marriage was not settlement and that the parties intend to live together permanently as husband and wife was clearly established.

(ii)   Following *Arun Kumar*, satisfying the burden of proof as far as intention to cohabit is concerned may cast 'a flood of light' on the question of primary purpose.

(iii)   Married applicants will be better off than fiancés to satisfy the immigration authorities about the genuineness of their application.

(iv)   The Rules examine the primary purpose of the marriage, not the reasons for the choice of a particular matrimonial home.

(v)   Entry clearance officers can legitimately bear in mind that it is less difficult to achieve an 'immigration marriage' under the South Asian arranged marriage system. Though greatest weight should be given to the intention of the applicant, in arranged marriage cases it is appropriate to look for the intentions of the spouses and those that arranged the marriage.

(vi)   Where a husband seeks to join his wife in the UK, this may well constitute a departure from traditional practice, but it does not mean that an inference of primary purpose should be drawn. Traditional South Asian customs were clearly modified in the context of transnational marriages, especially where the wife had a good position in the UK.

(vii)   Applicants who have sought settlement in the UK before marriage, who have been guilty of past immigration deception, or who have clearly stated that their main motive in marrying the sponsor was economic advancement or residence in the UK will have greater difficulty in discharging their burden of proof.

(viii)   The relevant date for assessment of primary purpose is the date of the decision, though assessment will be of the primary purpose as at the date of the marriage or proposed marriage, not at the date when the arrangements were made. There may be a change in the primary purpose between these various dates, though it remains to be seen how such evidence will be dealt with.

It is significant that a similar attempt to list principles or propositions was made in 1987 by the Court of Appeal in the case of *Hoque and Singh* ([1988] ImmAR 216) which we consider below.

Further clarification about situations in which applications would be refused was offered by the IAT in a number of reported cases. In *Afzal* (4784), which is reported as *Mohammad Afzal* v. *Visa Officer, Islamabad* at (1986) Imm AR 474, a young Pakistani man had originally made an application for entry clearance as a fiancé, but after refusal of the application and shortly before his appeal was heard by the IAT, the parties had married in Pakistan. The wife then returned to the UK after three months.

Before the IAT, the question of whether to consider the fact of this marriage or not inevitably arose. The determination, after sifting through the visa officer's explanatory statement and notes of interviews, comes down firmly against the couple's strategy:

'If Rehana had married the appellant some time ago and resided with him thereafter in Pakistan, this would no doubt have been very helpful, but this was not the case. She married him, remained in Pakistan for just over three months and then returned to this country. The marriage could be interpreted as an attempt to force the hand of the Home Office by presenting them with a *fait accompli.*' (p.479).

Nor was the IAT impressed with the 'intervening devotion' of this couple in the form of a few letters. At p.479 of the case it is stated that,

'Neither do we consider that the letters exchanged after the date of decision are of very great assistance.'

While emphasising that 'we have approached this case in the manner prescribed by the Master of the Rolls' (p.480) and almost apologetically pointing out that 'this is no doubt a borderline case' (p.480), this appeal was firmly dismissed. This decision was probably reached also because the wife was originally only 15 years old and, it appears, engaged to the appellant since childhood. Also, rather much was made in the interviews of the custom of following the husband's residence, and the case report contains much evidence of hostile questioning.

Other post-*Arun Kumar* decisions clearly indicated that the case-law was not going to assist all genuine marriages. Mole (1987:32) refers to the unreported case of *Gama Singh* (4902), where another fiancé application was superseded by marriage and the birth of a child. Despite this, the husband's application was refused and the IAT upheld the refusal, mainly because of damaging remarks made by the husband at interview. In *Kulwinder Singh* (4946) a husband's appeal was rejected for a number of reasons, but mainly because he had failed to show the 'intervening devotion' referred to in *Arun Kumar.*

Other reported cases at this time include the dismissed appeal of an Egyptian man who had a varied immigration history including a period of unlawful residence in Britain, whose marriage to a British citizen was suspected to be a marriage of convenience, and who was actually divorced by the time the Court of Appeal heard the case. Not surprisingly, in *Hisham Ahmed Ali Abdel Rahman* v. *The Secretary of State for the Home Department* ([1986] ImmAR 405), the Court of Appeal refused to entertain any thought of granting an application for indefinite leave to remain in the UK.

In *Ilyas Yacub Patel* v. *Secretary of State for the Home Department* ([1986] ImmAR 440), the appellant was an Indian Muslim man who had requested indefinite leave to remain, but whose marriage appeared to have broken down. In this case, the wife herself had stated that she did not wish the man to stay in this country or with her (p.441). There was some evidence that the marriage breakdown had been brought about by the overbearing attitudes of the woman's father, but the woman herself did not at all assist the man's case. Though the question of post-decision facts was prominently raised, the Tribunal ultimately came to a finding that already on the date of the refusal the wife no longer intended to live with the appellant permanently. Since the clear evidence was that one of the parties no longer had an intention of living with the other as his or her spouse, the man's application for indefinite leave to remain had to fail.

A probably typical case of a male applicant whose appeal is rejected because he stated frankly that he was keen to come to the UK is *Manjit Singh* v. *Entry Clearance Officer New Delhi* ([1986] ImmAR 219). Here the case report contains notes of the interview conducted in New Delhi, during which the appellant stated quite clearly that the marriage had been arranged so he could go to the UK (p.222). Focusing on the intentions of the appellant, the IAT found, at p.223, that:

'We do not think, on the evidence before us that there is any doubt that the appellant has chosen to accept the prospect of marriage to a divorced girl older than himself because of the opportunity that afforded him of gaining admission to and settlement in the United Kingdom. We come to that conclusion on the basis of his replies to questions fairly put to him by the entry clearance officer in the interview noted above.'

On the other hand, in *R.* v. *Immigration Appeal Tribunal ex parte Davesh Pranjivan Desai* ([1987] ImmAR 18) the applicant husband had expressly denied that he had married the sponsoring woman because he wanted to work and live in the United Kingdom (p.21), but he had been refused entry clearance under the primary purpose rule by an adjudicator. His application for leave to appeal to the IAT was rejected on the ground that there was no arguable point of law. However, Simon Brown J, in the Queen's Bench Division, found that the adjudicator had omitted to make any evaluation of the husband's own motives and had focused entirely on the evidence provided by several witnesses. Thus, the learned judge found:

'Of course, the purposes of those who arranged it are material and in the end may well be of conclusive importance. However, any decision which so wholly ignores, as this decision apparently ignores, any consideration of the applicant's own intentions of the matter, is in my judgement, insupportable.' (p.21).

There were other aspects of the adjudicator's decision which troubled Simon Brown J, *inter alia* that the adjudicator appeared to have placed 'too much reliance upon the mere fact that this was an arranged marriage' (p.22). Thus, it was held that:

'It is at least possible that the adjudicator here was in error in his approach to arranged marriages generally and that he arrived at too ready and bland a conclusion because the only essential findings of fact that he makes might well be thought essentially innocuous rather than adverse to the success of the application.' (p.22).

We see here also how the judgement of the Master of the Rolls in *Arun Kumar*, then just decided, had an instant effect on how Mr. Justice Simon Brown viewed the matter. This case was therefore referred back for a substantive appeal to the IAT.

A rather confused case is reported as *R. v. Immigration Appeal Tribunal ex parte Hardev Singh Dhillon* ([1987] ImmAR 385). Here the applicant, a young Sikh man from India, was technically a fiancé. His application for leave to enter the UK was refused because he had stated quite openly in the interview, through an interpreter, that he did not relish a future as a farmer and that both his brother's marriage to a girl in Canada and his own marriage arrangements with a girl from Britain had been made with the express purpose of emigration.

On appeal before the Queen's Bench Division, a number of procedural aspects were argued for this young man, and he was trying to retract damaging statements that he had made, but his application was firmly dismissed. What is interesting about this case is the way in which the couple ruined their own chances of success by rushing into arrangements, illustrating what Nuala Mole (1987:37) has been saying about the ill-advised.

Thus, it is not clear from the case report whether Stuart-Smith J, noticed the obvious distortion of South Asian legal matters that had a bearing on this case. His summary of the facts illustrates the need for 'ethnic training' for judges:

'A Miss Kaur was born in this country on 19 April 1965. A marriage was arranged between her and the applicant in about January 1982. Following that she visited India with her father and met the applicant and an engagement between them took place in April of 1982. It was celebrated by means of an exchange of gifts and it was agreed that the marriage would take place according to Sikh religious ceremonies. The marriage in fact did not take place because Miss Kaur was too young for a valid marriage under Indian law. But the parties lived together as man and wife between about 9 May 1982 and 6 September of that year.

When she returned to this country she was then pregnant and since then, of course, she has had a child.' (p.386).

137

A number of the facts so innocuously stated here require some critical comment. The whole case illustrates that fiancé applications are subject to more hazards than husband cases, confirming Ian Macdonald's point (iii) above (p.134). Delaying this application for a year might have made all the difference. The case also raises the question whether a more honest statement of the real situation would have allowed a line of argument that takes into account intervening devotion, which does not appear to arise in this case, probably because it was originally decided much before *Arun Kumar.*

What should have struck anybody dealing with this case, though, is the fact that an Asian woman is here presented as a fiancée, though she has been subjected to consummation of the marital relationship and has already born a child. The fact that the parties are Sikhs, people fiercely protective of the chastity of their women and of the notion of honour (*izzat*), has quite clearly been overlooked. It is totally implausible that this couple should be treated as engaged, when it seems certain that between some time in April 1982 and 9th May 1982 there was a full Sikh wedding, legitimising the consummation of the marriage.

The legal argument advanced to explain the decision not to marry, namely that the marriage of a 17 year old woman in India would be invalid, would be wrong under Indian Hindu law, which applies to Sikh marriages also. However, if we assume that the girl was a British citizen, her marriage would indeed need to be registered under the Indian *Special Marriage Act* of 1954 to give it full legal validity. This, clearly, would not have been possible till the girl had reached the age of 18 years.

If we therefore assume that the couple could not validly get married under the relevant Indian law, the technique chosen to get around this dilemma was to have a Sikh wedding only, which did not give legal validity to the marriage in the eyes of English law, nor of Indian law. The decision that the husband should apply as a fiancé is, thus, technically correct, but it perhaps deprived the couple of a better chance to be allowed to stay together in Britain.

The case report itself focuses only on various procedural aspects, but the man's application was refused since he stated his intentions of moving to Britain too unambiguously in response to questions by the entry clearance officer.

There will have been innumerable cases of this kind during the 1980s. It was becoming increasingly apparent to advisers and to South Asians themselves that there was a major dilemma in the application of the primary purpose rule: for a British-born Asian woman to state that she was prepared to stay with her fiancé or husband in the subcontinent evoked a response that then the man's application to come to the UK showed evidence of 'primary purpose'. On the other hand, where the woman made it a condition of the marriage arrangement that the couple should establish themselves in Britain, any man who sought to marry such a woman would be challenged as being primarily interested in settlement in Britain. Thus, the conundrum of deciding what the 'primary purpose' of an applicant may be continued without respite.

■ 4.8 Seeking to establish guidelines: Hoque and Singh

Nuala Mole, writing at a time when another important case had just begun to surface in reported form, seems to suggest that the courts appeared to take a more detached view of the Immigration Rules than the IAT (Mole 1987:32). Again, this observation points to evidence of growing discomfort in the higher judiciary about the human rights implications of the primary purpose rule, as reiterated more clearly a few years later by Rick Scannell (1992:3):

> 'It seemed (in a small way at least) that the judiciary were prepared to add their voice to the widespread and entirely justifiable condemnation and anger felt both by those affected by the operation of the rule and by practitioners trying to overcome its iniquities.'

In what has been called 'a rueful understatement' (Rees 1989:92), the Court of Appeal indicated in the important case of *Immigration Appeal Tribunal* v. *Amirul Hoque and Matwinder Singh* ([1988] ImmAR 216), the case of *Hoque and Singh*, that 'the application of the rules gives rise to some difficulties in practice' (p.220).

In this case, the Court of Appeal was again called into action after a decidedly pro-immigrant decision by Mr. Justice Simon Brown in the Queen's Bench Division which has remained unreported. As Rick Scannell (1992:3) has argued, this decision represented the high water mark of the earlier approach in *Arun Kumar* ([1986] ImmAR 446) that it would not make sense for a British-settled Asian woman wishing to stay in Britain to marry a man who was not prepared to come here. In *R*. v. *Immigration Appeal Tribunal ex parte Matwinder Singh* (The Times, 15 April 1987), decided on 23 March 1987, Simon Brown J had re-affirmed his trust in the genuine nature of most Asian marriage arrangements:

> 'In my judgement — and I have little doubt that this consideration informed the Master of Rolls' judgement in Kumar — it is necessary to recognise the intrinsic improbability that any two people, even from a culture where arranged marriages are the norm, will bind and commit themselves for life in marriage with all that implies primarily in order to achieve the husband's settlement in the United Kingdom.'

This dictum clearly constituted a potential and powerful threat to the effectiveness of the exclusionary mechanisms of the primary purpose rule. Thus, the Home Office appealed this decision, though it is stated in a more friendly manner in the headnote (p.216) that 'the Tribunal appealed and sought clarification generally of the relevant law.'

The respondents in these two cases were respectively citizens of Bangladesh and India, had both married women who were British citizens and had been refused leave to remain in the UK (Mr. Hoque) or leave to enter (Mr. Singh) as the immigration authorities were not satisfied that in each case the primary purpose of the marriage had not been for the husband to obtain settlement in the UK. Their appeals to adjudicators had been dismissed, leave to appeal to the IAT had been refused, but both were successful on application for judicial review.

The facts of the cases are very briefly stated at p. 218 of the case, are separately given in more detail for *Hoque* at pp. 225-226 and for *Singh* at pp. 229-231, but they are not material here. The importance of *Hoque and Singh* lies in that it was, again, a test case in which the position of the two men involved was of much less concern than the principles used in making decisions. Again, the court was told that there were a number of other pending cases in which similar problems are raised (p.219).

Slade LJ, who delivered the judgement of the Court of Appeal, first turned to the relevant Rules under HC 169, Rule 41 dealing with fiancés, Rule 54 for husbands, and Rule 126 for extensions of stay. He discerned the broad object of these Rules, inferring that:

> 'It is to prevent a man from obtaining leave to enter or remain in the United Kingdom in his capacity as the husband of a woman settled here in cases either where the marriage was in the first place not a genuine marriage but a device to enable him to achieve leave to enter or remain in this country or where the parties to the marriage no longer intend (even if they previously intended) to live together permanently as man and wife.' (p.220).

The Court then turned to its decisions in *Bhatia* and *Arun Kumar*, stated that both decisions were binding on it, and that only one important sentence of Sir John Donaldson MR in *Arun Kumar* had been *obiter*. This was then swiftly followed by listing a series of propositions of law 'which we think are clearly to be derived from one or both of those decisions' (p.220). These propositions (fully formulated at pp.220-222, in short form listed at pp. 216-217 of the case report) should be considered in marriage cases (Shutter 1992:29) and are, in essence, as follows:

1. The onus of proof under rule 41, on the balance of probabilities, falls on the applicant.

2. Similarly, under rule 54 the onus falls upon the applicant to show that, at the time when the marriage took place, its primary purpose was not to obtain admission to the UK.

3. In considering an application under either rule, the entry clearance officer is not limited to such evidence as the applicant may put before him.

4. While the applicant's intention is the central consideration, the intention of both parties will be relevant; in an arranged marriage, also the reasons of those who arranged the marriage will be relevant.

5. The mere fact that rule 41(b) is satisfied does not by itself suffice to enable an applicant to satisfy rule 41(a).

6. Similarly, satisfaction of rule 54(b) does not of itself mean satisfaction of rule 54(a). It must be borne in mind that rule 54(a) looks at intention at the date of the marriage, while rule 41(a) is looking at intention at the present time.

7. An applicant who satisfies paragraphs (b) and (c) under rules 41 and 54 is better placed to satisfy the respective paragraph (a). This goes more so for rule 54, where 'evidence bearing on one question will often cast a flood of light on the other'.

8. Where arranged marriages are the norm, while relevant, the fact that a particular marriage is arranged does not show that its purpose is or was to obtain admission to the UK. The intention to make a true and lasting marriage may be formed after only a short acquaintance, different from a couple belonging to a Western community.

9. The factum of application for entry clearance under rule 41 or 54 usually presupposes an intention to settle in the UK. Thus, it is 'fatally easy' but wrong to treat an applicant's admission that he seeks settlement in the UK as evidence of the primary purpose of the marriage.

10. The propositions set out above must equally apply to rule 126 of HC 169.

Next the Court turned to the one controversial sentence in the case of *Arun Kumar*, which had given rise to the present appeals. Slade LJ, reiterating the finding of Nourse LJ that the adjudicator in *Arun Kumar* had failed to have due regard to propositions 7 and 8 above, then turned to what Sir John Donaldson MR had said:

'For my part I do not think that any violence would be done to this country's immigration policy if entry clearance officers put out of their minds the theoretical possibility that a marriage which at the time of application is, on the evidence, undoubtedly a very genuine and soundly based marriage could, at its inception some time before, have had a different character.' (p.224).

Macdonald and Blake (1991:262) have commented on this, saying that the Master of the Rolls,

'contrasted 'genuine' and 'immigration' marriages, and made the suggestion that if a marriage was soundly based, the possibility of its failing the primary purpose test was only theoretical and such a theory could in practice be ignored by the ECO... The ultimate test was what was the real or fundamental purpose of the marriage, and only if cohabitation was entirely subsidiary could the spouse be excluded.'

The Court of Appeal in *Hoque and Singh* interpreted the words of the Master of the Rolls as a piece of advice to entry clearance officers to the effect that, where at the time of the application the marriage is clearly genuine and soundly based, 'they need feel under no obligation to 'scratch around' for evidence tending to show that at the time when it was entered into its primary purpose was to obtain admission to the United Kingdom.' (p.225).

Thus, at first sight, the Court of Appeal in *Hoque and Singh* saw no reason to differ from the advice offered by the Master of the Rolls in *Arun Kumar* and found it 'to accord with common sense and humanity' (p.225). But this apparently liberal stance was immediately nullified by Slade LJ:

'However, in the end, it must be left to entry clearance officers to decide how they do their work.' (p.225).

This was explained as meaning that, even in a case where the marriage was shown to be genuine and soundly based at the date of the application, entry clearance officers were neither precluded from making enquiries into the circumstances of the marriage arrangements, nor were they entitled to shut their eyes to evidence that the marriage may not satisfy the requirements of paragraph (a) in rule 41, 54 or 126. In other words, the Court of Appeal did not challenge, in principle, the power of the entry clearance officers to exercise their subjective discretion in making decisions about the question of primary purpose.

The considerable anxiety of the Home Office that the discretionary powers of entry clearance officers and adjudicators might be curtailed by the case law emanating from the Court of Appeal shines through at p. 235 of the judgement in *Hoque and Singh*, where Slade LJ seems to assure the Tribunal that there could never again be a shift in the burden of proof to the entry clearance officer. Mr. Justice Simon Brown may have rocked the conscience of the Court of Appeal, but that was as far as one could go without endangering the policy aims of British immigration control. Though we now have the ten propositions, which Rees (1989:92) has described as 'settled law', the primary purpose rule itself remained virtually untouched. As Sue Shutter (1992:25) most recently expressed it,

'...if rigidly applied, it is almost impossible for an applicant to prove a negative intention — that a marriage did not take place primarily for immigration reasons — when the foreign spouse is in fact applying to enter the UK and comes from a country with a lower per capita income than the UK, or a community with a history of immigration to the UK.'

The decision in Hoque and Singh, thus, though it appeared to come down in favour of the two applicants, did not ultimately help spouses caught up in this rule. On the other hand, as Griffith (1991:184) has pointed out, it emphasised again that the genuineness of a marriage must have an important bearing on the question of primary purpose. Macdonald and Blake (1991:262) use the image of reaching a watershed:

'The Home Office had established that primary purpose and intention to cohabit were distinct requirements and that a marriage could fail one but succeed in the other; immigrants had established that primary purpose could not be analysed independently of the intent to cohabit.'

The subsequent case-law demonstrates how the judiciary has been unable to avoid falling into a trap of its own making and now finds itself inextricably involved in arguments about fine points which seem rather academic, while at the same time showing no real inclination to relate this discussion to the suffering of applicants and their spouses and families who are caught up in the 'no-win situation'.

Much attention has been focused on proposition 7 in *Hoque and Singh*, concerning the relationship of a finding that a marriage is genuine and intended to be permanent on the one hand, and the question of primary purpose, on the other. In *R. v. Immigration Appeal Tribunal ex parte Bashir*, an unreported decision (15 March 1988) by Hodgson J in the Divisional Court, it was held that proposition 7 places upon an ECO and an adjudicator the obligation to consider first whether the marriage is genuine and intended to be permanent:

'It places upon an ECO and an adjudicator the obligation to consider the requirements of sub-paragraphs (b) and (c) before he considers sub-paragraph (a). Without doing that, he cannot be in a position to see whether, and to what degree of illumination, light is cast on (a) by (b) and (c).' (cited by Rees 1989:93).

This interpretation may seem sensible and in line with common sense. However, as Rees (1989) points out and illustrates with examples, mainly from unreported cases, there was obvious disagreement between first instance judges on whether adjudicators or ECOs should make specific findings on the permanency of a relationship before making up their mind about primary purpose.

Griffith (1991:185 n.70) refers to three other cases in which this appears to have been a central point. It is an important issue, as Rees argues, because a finding that a permanent union is not established may be challengeable as unreasonable and would make a consequent finding on primary purpose reviewable. On the other hand, as Rees (1989:93) also argues,

'a positive finding on permanency coupled with a negative finding on purpose may, depending on the circumstances, make the decision irrational.'

This is clearly a very important issue. It seeks to control the discretion of the immigration officers to the extent that they cannot simply record their opinion that a particular marriage was entered into primarily for the purpose of entry or settlement. This point now began to arise when it was unclear from the determination itself whether an adjudicator had followed the correct *Hoque and Singh* approach. The correctness of an adjudicator's approach may only be ascertained, as some judges were trying to argue, if there was evidence that paragraphs (b) and (c) had in fact been considered before (a). This point was raised in *R. v. Immigration Appeal Tribunal ex parte Vijay Kumar*, decided on 23 February 1989 by Mr. Justice Kennedy who held that,

'..in any ordinary case if nothing is said about the requirements of (b) or about the evidence relating to those requirements, it may be very difficult for a court to be satisfied that the adjudicator has taken all relevant matters into consideration.' (cited at Rees 1989:93).

In *R. v. Immigration Appeal Tribunal ex parte Sudash Bala Garg* (The Times, 17 March 1989), the same judge allowed another application for judicial review because there was no specific finding on the permanency of the marriage (Rees 1989:93-94). This clearly meant that entry clearance officers could not openly say that they had preconceived notions about 'immigration marriages'. Certainly, an adjudicator's failure to have regard to material facts could result in the decision being set aside or referred back for further consideration (Griffith 1991:185).

In this context, we need to emphasise again how large the share of immigration cases in judicial review has gradually become. The intense struggle over how to apply the *Hoque and Singh* propositions had to lead to still further litigation and frustrated the earlier hope (see Scannell 1992:3) of a reduction in the number of cases in this area of law.

In some cases, it was less difficult for the courts to reach a negative decision, but one can also read in them evidence of growing judicial hostility to primary purpose applicants. Thus, in *Pervez Iqbal* v. *Immigration Appeal Tribunal* ([1988] ImmAR 469), a fiancé application from Pakistan, it was found by May LJ that there had been a previous, allegedly fraudulent attempt to get the applicant into the UK as a young boy. It should be noted that the judge seems extremely wary of this and goes even to the extent of blaming the applicant for the fact that his earlier application was delayed over more than four years (p.471).

The sponsor, who had grown up in Pakistan and in Birmingham, had stated her unwillingness to settle in Pakistan. The parties had in fact got married during the pendency of the proceedings. While we find no negative comments on the lines of 'forcing the hand of the court' by this marriage, the court is totally unwilling to even consider the genuineness of the marriage. In view of the past immigration history of the man, May LJ found the evidence of the woman unreliable, her arguments against living in Pakistan 'nebulous' (p.471), and he held that the adjudicator had had enough evidence before him to come to the reasonable conclusion that,

'by hook or by crook the sponsor and her father are determined to get the boy into the United Kingdom by the only means open to them.' (p.472).

In this case, an attempt was made to rely on the situation of a girl from the UK who is unwilling to stay with her husband in Pakistan and who is 'in somewhat of a Catch 22 situation':

'If she says that she does want to marry the potential immigrant but wants to marry him and continue to live in this country, where she was born, whose passport she holds and where she is presently living, then care must be taken not to jump to the inference without more that the primary purpose of the intended marriage is to facilitate the entry of the immigrant.' (p.472).

However, as we saw, there was enough accumulated weight against the applicant and his sponsors in this outrightly unsympathetic determination.

An equally unhelpful and more subtly hostile case is *R. v. Immigration Appeal Tribunal ex parte Sukhjivan Singh* ([1988] ImmAR 527), in which Mr. Justice Simon Brown, sitting in the Queen's Bench Division, indicates some judicial irritation with the constant workload of primary purpose cases. This is indeed evidence, as Scannell (1992:3) has pointed out, of 'a perceptible shift of sympathy by the judiciary'. Simon Brown J started his judgement as follows:

'This is another application for judicial review arising out of the vexed primary purpose rules'. (p.527).

The case focused attention on the adjudicator's finding of a genuine marriage, which had been coupled with adverse comments on the speed with which the marriage had been arranged and had led to a refusal of the man's application for indefinite leave to remain.

The applicant in this case had come to the UK in August 1985 as a visitor, claiming that he had come to attend his sister's marriage and that he himself was due to marry a girl in India later in the year. Having obtained one month's leave to enter, he then asked for an extension of three months, which was granted. Meanwhile, in September, he met the sponsor, they were attracted to each other, got engaged in October, registered their marriage on 16 November 1985 and had a Sikh religious wedding on 1 December 1985.

In what the judge calls 'a long and careful determination' (p.528), the adjudicator had set out the evidence before her. Basically, she distrusted the appellant and found him 'devious' (p.529) and prepared to lie. A catalogue of negative evidence against the man's credibility is listed, including the fact that he had claimed to wish to come to the UK for the marriage of his sister, when she was in fact a cousin (p.529). It was apparently not pointed out to the adjudicator, nor to Simon Brown J, that Sikhs (like many other South Asians) commonly refer to first cousins as 'sisters' or 'brothers', so here rather much is made of a cultural matter that is insensitively and aggressively weighted against the applicant.

The adjudicator, an upper-class white woman, was evidently unable and unwilling to accept that a Sikh arranged marriage could be finalised within a few weeks. Though she was prepared to accept that this was a genuine marriage, she nevertheless objected to it on a variety of grounds:

'I do not accept that this speed was normal... I find the wedding arrangements were made at such speed so they could marry and be able to be living together as man and wife before the appellant's leave to be here as a visitor expired.' (p.529).

Though the adjudicator was aware of the decisions in *R. v. Immigration Appeal Tribunal ex parte Lunat*, an unreported decision (6 October 1986) of the

Queen's Bench Division, and of the Master of the Rolls' speech in *Arun Kumar* ([1986] ImmAR 446), and though she saw the couple happily living together a year after the marriage, she had come to the conclusion that the matrimonial relationship was only of secondary importance and that the primary purpose of the marriage in this case was to enable the husband to extend his stay in the UK.

This seemed like an irrational finding in view of the clear statement that this was a genuine marriage. It was challenged by the applicant's barrister, who focused on the adjudicator's earlier finding that the marriage was genuine and on the relationship between such a finding and a conclusion about primary purpose. If she had so clearly seen a genuine marriage, how could it then become an 'immigration' marriage falling down on primary purpose? Simon Brown J found himself unwilling to accept this argument and, in essence, confirmed what advisers know well, namely that rushing into a marriage may ruin the case altogether. It was held that this particular marriage 'was entered into in circumstances which raised obvious doubts as to its true underlying purpose' (p.533) and the application was dismissed.

Macdonald and Blake (1991:262-263), too, have emphasised that a whole set of cases at this time turned on the question whether a distinct finding on the genuineness of the marriage is necessary before a decision on primary purpose is reached. In *R. v. Immigration Appeal Tribunal ex parte Khatab* ([1989] ImmAR 313), Henry J ruled that a specific and unambiguous finding on the genuineness of a marriage was in most cases a necessary foundation for the examination of its primary purpose. In *R. v. Immigration Appeal Tribunal ex parte Shameem Wali* ([1989] ImmAR 86), Mr. Justice Farquharson, in the Queen's Bench Division, commented:

'If one is considering a case under paragraph (a), then paragraph (b) is always relevant. It may be it is of relative insignificance if the evidence available to the entry clearance officer is precisely the same under both (a) and (b). But if the evidence between the two is different so that, for example, different conclusions could be arrived at, whether favourably or otherwise, for the applicant in those circumstances, the conclusion on (b) will be significant when the adjudicator or entry clearance officer turns his mind to (a). There are cases where the evidence available will result in the same answer to both (a) and (b), and, therefore, the determination of (a) necessarily involves determination of (b). But there are, of course, many more where the decision made on paragraph (b) will be in favour of the applicant and that on (a) against him. Accordingly, in my judgement, the applicant is entitled to be informed of those findings.'

Though the conclusion in this case was not favourable to the applicant, since the judge found that the evidence on both requirements was the same, this judicial statement posed a further potential threat to the range of discretion of entry clearance officers and adjudicators.

Though, as Rees (1989:93-94) and Macdonald and Blake (1991:263) show, the above position was by no means an agreed one, the Home Office was sufficiently worried to attempt behind-the-scenes activities to protect the primary purpose rule; these were constitutionally quite unacceptable (see Macdonald and Blake 1991:263). The alternative strategy, namely to appeal some of the decisions, was apparently not taken. This shows, perhaps, some distrust of the higher judiciary. Could they possibly turn pro-immigrant and ruin the finely woven net that caught most South Asian spouses?

Despite such worries, any attempt to get rid of the primary purpose rule altogether would be doomed to failure from the outset. The courts have clearly not been prepared to dismantle the primary purpose rule altogether. In a predictably vain attempt (Rees 1989:92) to persuade the Court of Appeal that the primary purpose rule is 'outrageous and uncertain', and therefore *ultra vires* (Rees 1989:92), *Yogeshkumar Shantilal Rajput* v. *Immigration Appeal Tribunal* ([1989] ImmAR 350) did not have a satisfactory outcome.

In this case, the facts are really straightforward. A young Asian woman from Leicester in the UK had been taken to India by her parents to marry a young man there on 21 January 1983. The husband immediately applied for entry clearance, the wife returned to the UK on 27 February, and the husband was interviewed in Bombay. One notes that the case report (p.352) misrepresents 'the appellant's dialect is Gujerati', whereas the correct statement would have been that the interview was conducted through an interpreter in Gujarati, which is one of the officially recognised major languages of India.

Having been refused by the ECO on 28 March 1984, the husband found his appeal to an adjudicator in Birmingham dismissed on 21 March 1986. The appellant was then granted leave to move for judicial review on 11 November 1986 and McNeill J heard his case in the Divisional Court on 22 March 1988, dismissing the application. On appeal to the Court of Appeal it was submitted (p.352) that rule 54(a), i.e. the primary purpose rule,

'is partial and unequal in its operation, is manifestly unjust and involves an outrageous interference with the rights of those subject to it... it is so outrageous that it is possible to say that Parliament never intended to authorise the making of such a rule.'

It was further submitted (p.352) that this rule was *ultra vires* section 3(2) of the *Immigration Act*, 1971 and that such a rule could not really be 'lawfully imposed on any person' in accordance with section 1(1) of that Act. In the alternative, the appellant also invited the court to find that the adjudicator's decision had not been in accordance with the guidelines given by the Master of the Rolls in *Arun Kumar* ([1986] ImmAR 446).

The Court of Appeal found that HC 169 of 1983, which contained the relevant rule, has the implicit authority of Parliament 'in the sense that no resolution was passed negativing the rule or seeking to alter it' (p.354). The Court then went through its own judgements in *Bhatia, Arun Kumar* and *Hoque and Singh* before turning its attention to the 'interesting argument' (p.358) developed by Counsel that the primary purpose rule was *ultra vires* and that Parliament could not have intended that the rule should be made in such terms under the *Immigration Act*, 1971. The argument, in essence, was that,

> '...it was difficult if not impossible to conceive of a person marrying a British spouse and wishing to live in the United Kingdom actually succeeding in discharging the burden of proving that settlement in the United Kingdom was not a primary purpose of the marriage since... the immigration officer or entry clearance officer... could within the terms of the rules always decide that he is 'not satisfied' by reason merely of the fact of the proposed settlement.'(p.358).

It was submitted that this was particularly the case where the wife had been born in England and wanted her husband to live with her in the UK. The rule was 'a serious manifestation of unfairness' (p.360) and 'amounted in practice to a permanent bar upon the applicant and his wife once the ruling had been made' (p.360). The primary purpose rule, it was argued, thus had the effect of leading to the break-up of family life, which was 'clearly contrary to the public policy which seeks to uphold the state of matrimony' (p.358). Any rule seeking to exclude partners to genuine marriages 'must of itself be considered to be unreasonable' (p.358).

The rule was also challenged on the ground that it is 'selective, divisive and unfair because it is clearly aimed at those who come from the third world' (p.358). The rule was historically designed to deal with marriages of convenience, and 'it was in itself unfair to require an applicant to prove a negative' (p.358).

The primary purpose rule was defended by Counsel for the Secretary of State as a 'logical policy' (p.359) and it was repeatedly asserted that there was no uncertainty in the terms of this rule, which can well be taken and read as a cynical assumption of power. It was also said that 'there was no question of preventing the parties living together but only of preventing them from living together in England' (p.360) and the argument of a permanent bar was, obviously, not agreed to, though no detailed reasons were given.

Sir Stephen Brown, the President of the Court of Appeal, stated clearly that the Court had the power to hold that the challenged rule was *ultra vires* (p.359). He found the argument advanced for the appellant 'ingenious' (p.360), wondered why it had not been brought before the Court on a previous occasion, and declared himself satisfied that his court had now been able to consider the rule 'with care and in the light of very detailed and helpful arguments'. But he nevertheless stated tersely (at p. 360):

> 'I am not prepared to hold that the rule is *ultra vires*.'

This almost obstinate refusal to acknowledge and recognise the possibility of human suffering in the name of the law is, in remarkably similar terms, continued in the consideration of the second limb of the argument. Here we see that already the adjudicator had asserted that he had 'carefully considered' (p.360) all the evidence before he came to his negative conclusions.

What the adjudicator had had before him was clear evidence of a situation, all too common, where the girl had made it a condition of the marriage that the boy joined her in the UK, despite the fact that he had a reasonably good job in India. The case report shows very clearly that there were a number of considerations that motivated the man to agree to marrying a girl from Britain, but the adjudicator decided that the 'major intention in the marriage was to go to England' (p.362).

It must be noted that the adjudicator had even tried to wriggle out of the primary purpose conundrum by studiously avoiding the term, speaking of 'major intention' rather than 'primary purpose' and introducing also the term 'essential consideration' (p.361). The adjudicator, finding himself in agreement with the entry clearance officer about the evaluation of the evidence, had simply said that the ECO had 'no axe to grind' (p.362) and upheld his decision.

The President explicitly declared himself satisfied that the decision of the adjudicator 'reveals a close attention to all the relevant facts' (p.363) and that the adjudicator has — again we note that the magic word appears — approached his task 'carefully and independently'.

The brief separate judgement by Glidewell LJ discloses no material difference of opinion, but it emphasises, in a significant way, that the wife had no intention of settling in India (p.365). It almost seems as though for Asian women resident in Britain to state this intention openly and make the consequent condition to their partner in an arranged marriage is vigorously objected to by Glidewell LJ.

After *Rajput*, one must be left to draw the conclusion that the primary purpose rule is there to stay as an integral element of British immigration control, and that the judges are unwilling to interfere significantly in this control mechanism.

■ 4.9 The waning of judicial sympathy

After the almost quixotic attempt in *Rajput* to get rid of the primary purpose rule altogether, one may discern a backlash on several fronts. Firstly, though it is impossible to prove, the decision in *Rajput* will have emboldened entry clearance officers who, despite liberal court decisions, as Rick Scannell (1992:3) has observed, 'frequently continued (as they do today) to approach decision taking in a cynical and uninformed manner'. Similarly adjudicators, provided they *appear* to follow the propositions of *Hoque and Singh*, will feel safe in rejecting many applications on entirely subjective criteria because the law allows them to do this, and some of the more recent decisions will 'ring loudest in adjudicators' ears' (Scannell 1990:147).

Among the higher judiciary, on the surface it looks as though judicial impatience with the primary purpose rule has grown. Rick Scannell (1992:3) has certainly captured the new flavour when he notes growing evidence of judicial impatience and a sense of disappointment with the continuing flood of judicial review cases on primary purpose. It seems, however, that something else has happened as well. Once the Court of Appeal had been openly confronted with the full horrors of the primary purpose rule, and the Court had equally openly declared its inability to help applicants, further action seems almost pointless in many cases. One could say that the courts are tired of primary purpose appeals, but they have also developed a new restrictive approach which, as we shall see, signals the limits of domestic remedies for applicants and makes life even harder, not only for South Asian males, but also for other groups of applicants that may now fall under the primary purpose rule.

After the strong indication by Glidewell LJ in *Rajput* v. *Immigration Appeal Tribunal* ([1989 ImmAR 350, at 365) that British Asian women could not just put conditions of choice of residence on their spouses, this has now become a major issue in the case law. Macdonald and Blake (1991:263) detected this as a new trend. Their balanced discussion of the issue, reflecting a wide diversity of judicial opinion on this question, needs now to be supplemented by reference to more recent cases, which have become decidedly hostile to immigrants. In *R.* v. *Immigration Appeal Tribunal ex parte Shameen Wali* ([1989] ImmAR 86), Farquharson in the Queen's Bench Division, had still commented:

'There is no reason why a British citizen, a woman, living in this country, should not wish to make it a condition of her marrying that she would only do so to somebody who, like herself, was going to live in the United Kingdom.' (p.91).

Farquharson J, therefore, found it proper that such a woman should take the attitude that she does not wish to live elsewhere, an approach which seems to give a right to British-based Asian women to choose their future matrimonial home before they choose their husband. This approach, as we have seen, was not shared by Glidewell LJ at p.365 in *Rajput*, which is now cited by Macdonald and Blake (1991:263) as the authority for the restrictive view.

The argument about choice of residence developed not directly, but in the context of the relationship between paragraphs (b) and (a) of the relevant Immigration Rules, i.e. the question whether a finding on genuineness has to be made before a decision is reached on primary purpose. In the Court of Appeal case of *Kandiya and Khan,* cited as *Naushad Khandia* v. *Immigration Appeal Tribunal* and *Aurangzeb Khan* v. *Immigration Appeal Tribunal* ([1990] ImmAR 377), the liberal approach of the earlier unreported decision in *Bashir* (see above p.143) and of *R.* v. *Immigration Appeal Tribunal ex parte Khatab* ([1989] ImmAR 313) was rejected. It was held that under proposition 7 of *Hoque and Singh* it was not necessary as a matter of law that there was a specific finding on genuineness before primary purpose could be considered, as long as the adjudicator gave adequate reasons for his decision. Thus the irrational view, obviously favoured by the Home Office, that a marriage may be declared perfectly genuine, but could still fall down under the primary purpose rule, was strengthened.

In *Kandiya and Khan*, the common complaint on appeal was that following the 10 propositions laid down in *Hoque and Singh* ([1988] ImmAR 216), it was the duty of an adjudicator in a primary purpose case to make a finding as to the genuineness of the marriage before considering the question of primary purpose, and this had not been done.

Taylor LJ in his judgement found that the propositions 'do not demand as a matter of law a specific finding as to (b) before proceeding to (a)' (p.380) and agreed, at p. 385, with Simon Brown J in *R. v. Immigration Appeal Tribunal ex parte Naushad Kandiya* ([1989] ImmAR 491) that:

'I believe the correct approach to be to consider these adjudications sensibly and realistically in the light of the particular matters in issue, not to require adjudicators in their decision making to follow slavishly some pre-ordained route, let alone to recite routinely as an incantation certain particular assumptions or conclusions which could well be implied in their decisions.'

While the legal argument is centred on this particular issue, it must be emphasised that the substantive facts of Kandiya focus attention on the freedom of British Asian women to choose a suitable spouse for themselves from anywhere in the world. In this case, a Ugandan Asian woman settled in Britain, having been unsuccessful in finding a husband in Britain, had gone to India for this purpose. The young Indian man she selected was seven years younger, the arrangements were made with considerable speed, and the woman was quite adamant that she would not wish to live in India. All this, together with the fact that the man might expect economic advantages in entering the UK, led to the refusal of the application. It is remarkable indeed that the entry clearance officer, as reported at p. 383 of the judgement, considered only the position of the man, when it was so very obvious from the facts before him that the primary purpose of the marriage was to find a husband for the British-based woman.

In *Aurangzeb Khan*, the second case of *Kandiya and Khan*, the sponsor was a young Pakistani-born woman who was now settled in Birmingham, had become a British citizen, and had got engaged to a young man during a prolonged visit to Pakistan in early 1984. Apparently, the question of settlement of the couple had not been properly discussed, though there seemed to be an assumption that the girl did not want to live in Pakistan. The young man, who also claimed to love her, 'wanted to come to the United Kingdom for her sake' (p.386).

The entry clearance officer and the adjudicator found it quite simple, in this situation, to pick up discrepancies and to come to an adverse conclusion on primary purpose, which was accepted as appropriate by the Court of Appeal.

In *Mohamed Numanul Islam Choudhury* v. *Immigration Appeal Tribunal* ([1990] ImmAR 211), the Court of Appeal declined to come to the assistance of a young Bangladeshi couple, despite the 'elliptical' nature of the decision (p.218) and the birth of a child. Here, the vexed issue of discrepancies and repeated reference to lies being told damaged the case beyond retrieval. There were some sympathetic comments, however, the legal technicalities are quite clearly weighted against the appellant.

Where a couple is not clear about the long-term intentions of settlement, as many are, the judges appear to assume that this is such a central issue that an absence of clear admission of the wish to settle in Britain, or any form of discrepancy must be weighted against the applicant's credibility. This is unsatisfactory, since it assumes (i) that settlement is the major issue, whereas it is only one of many and (ii) that Britain is necessarily the preferred destination. It does not appear to have occurred to the courts that well-off persons in Pakistan, India or Bangladesh would certainly have a much more comfortable life than they would in Britain. Where spouses in an interview voice uncertainty about their choice of matrimonial home, the courts should be careful not to adopt a blindly one-sided approach to this question.

An example of careful application of mind to this issue is found in *R. v. Immigration Appeal Tribunal ex parte Najma Rafique* ([1990] ImmAR 235). Here, a young fiancé from Pakistan had been unwilling or unable to say during the interview by the entry clearance officer how long he intended to remain in the UK after the proposed marriage. The man's response, when pressed, that 'I will do whatever she tells me to do' (p.238) led to a straightforward refusal of entry clearance.

In the Queen's Bench Division, Simon Brown J emphasised that the main problem was that 'the applicant cannot say what his long-term intentions are' (p.236). This indecision not only led to refusal, but also to the argument that he was outside the Immigration Rules, which require an applicant to be either a fiancé or husband, or a visitor. The case report provides ample evidence of the entry clearance officer expecting the man to make up his mind, but he continues to say that he will do what his future wife decides, arguing that this can be discussed only after marriage (pp.237-238).

The Tribunal had referred to other cases in which there was a similar situation. From the unreported decision of *Sukhinder Singh* (5329), it is obvious that counsel for the appellant had pointed out that the Immigration Rules did not adequately cover the class of persons who were undecided as to settlement after marriage (p.239). However, the Tribunal, aware that there may well be people who were genuinely undecided (p.239), saw indecision as prevarication, and as damaging to the applicant's case.

It appears that also in 1988, in the unreported case of *Syed Jabar Hussain Shah* (6033), a differently constituted panel of the IAT had taken a different view of the matter, acknowledging the dilemma:

> 'We see no purpose in failing to recognise that a person marrying another settled in this country may be exceedingly uncertain as to whether this country offers all that he or she hopes.... to force an applicant to state whether he intends to live here forever or for a period of not less than 6 months, invites deceit. It also seems to us to be somewhat removed from reality.' (p.240).

Considering the meaning of 'settlement' as explained by the Court of Appeal in *Rashida Bibi* v. *Immigration Appeal Tribunal* (1988] ImmAR 298), Simon Brown J found in *R.* v. *Immigration Appeal Tribunal ex parte Najma Rafique* ([1990] ImmAR 235) that the problem of categorising an uncertain application was actually resolved (p.241). Undecided applicants clearly fell under the category of fiancé or spouse. He thus proceeded to remit the appeal to the adjudicator, since it appeared that the question of primary purpose had not even been decided in the present case.

Macdonald and Blake (1991:263-264) comment on this case that:

'Spouses (or intending spouses) do not have to be certain that a permanent stay in the UK is intended before they are eligible for consideration as spouses as opposed to visitors, though feigned uncertainty may lead to an adverse finding on credibility.'

This position would appear to suggest that it is better for spouses to try and make up their minds about this issue as part of the marriage arrangements. However, the big question then becomes again whether a British-based Asian woman can dictate the terms of settlement, as the fiancé of Najma Rafique seemed to accept.

There are a few reported cases which were not decided against husbands from the subcontinent. Rick Scannell (1990) has discussed in some detail what Mr. Justice Judge said on 16 March 1990 in the Divisional Court in the unreported case of *Matwinder Singh*. Here, a young Sikh couple became engaged while the woman was on a visit to India in early 1983. The man applied for entry clearance as a fiancé immediately after the engagement. A few months later, the woman went back to India and the couple got married on 8 May 1983. Very soon, the wife was pregnant and returned to the UK, where a daughter was born. The husband's application was refused and in due course the IAT, in a determination of 31 October 1988 (6136), came to consider the case. The Tribunal directed itself to apply the relevant propositions and made some interesting observations:

'We are also aware of the danger that, having dealt with cases involving this question on an almost daily basis for the past five years, we may tend to consider the matter with somewhat jaded eyes. We have therefore been at pains to consider the question through the liberal spectacles now prescribed by their Lordships.' (cited by Scannell 1990:147).

Nevertheless, the Tribunal saw so many negative aspects of this case that they found themselves,

'...unable in all conscience to find that the appellant had discharged the onus relating to the purpose of the marriage.' (Scannell 1990:148).

In the Divisional Court, Judge J emphasised that the Court of Appeal had given clear guidance about the proper approach to cases where the marriage had been found to be genuine and solid. He stated that in such cases the IAT must analyse the material before it with great care. He found himself not impressed with the

153

reasoning of the Tribunal, detected several allegations that were shaky, to say the least, and thus quashed the Tribunal's dismissal of the husband's appeal. This case clearly shows that an unbiased approach is still possible, but is becoming increasingly rare.

In *R. v. Immigration Appeal Tribunal ex parte Kulbander Kaur* ([1990] ImmAR 107), McCullough J was asked to consider the refusal by an adjudicator of a young Sikh man, who had originally come to the UK as a visitor and had then married a British Sikh girl while she was on a visit to India. There was a clear finding of a genuine marriage, but the adjudicator had considered the economic motive of the applicant, the pattern of emigration in the family 'and the creditworthiness of the applicant, whom he disbelieved' (p.109). In the end, 'he came to the conclusion that he could not be satisfied that the applicant's primary purpose was not to obtain admission to this country' (p.109).

Mr. Justice McCullough in the Queen's Bench Division, though, was not prepared simply to dismiss the case. Untruths there had been, but there was also clear evidence of intervening devotion, and the adjudicator jumped to conclusions rather too fast, while,

'... there is nothing to show that the adjudicator appreciated the possible injustice of taking the step he apparently did.' (p. 110).

Rick Scannell, in Vol. 6 No.3 (1992) of *Immigration and Nationality Law and Practice*, p. 106 has briefly reported about another successful case, *Shaukat Ali*, in the Divisional Court, decided on 13 February 1992. Here, Kennedy J quashed the decision of the Tribunal because despite a genuine marriage, the birth of a daughter and intervening devotion it was simply asserted that all this did not cast a flood of light on the question of primary purpose. Again, the outcome of this case shows that a too bold assertion of the discretion granted to immigration officers is still subject to judicial censure.

Rick Scannell (1992:4-5) has also provided details of an interesting, then unreported Scottish case in which an applicant from Pakistan had been candid about his own wish to leave Pakistan and his assumption that the couple would settle in the United Kingdom. Lord Prosser, in *Mohammed Safter* v. *Secretary of State for the Home Department* ([1992] ImmAR 1), a case decided on 21 February 1991 in the Scottish Court of Session, took a remarkably open-minded view of the facts before him and came to the conclusion that an applicant's frank admission of the wish to settle in the UK need not be fatal to the application. Looking at the applicant's answers to questions put to him in interview, Lord Prosser found:

'If the parties were to marry, they would plainly have to agree where to live, and they had agreed to live in the United Kingdom. I see nothing sinister in that question and answer. So far as the remaining questions are concerned, they show that he had for some time wanted to leave Pakistan anyway. That explains his willingness to go along with the sponsor's insistence that they would have to live in the United Kingdom if they married.' (p.7).

Lord Prosser also found that the remaining answers,

'could no doubt be given by a person whose primary purpose in marrying was to obtain admission to the United Kingdom. But they could also, and equally, be given by a person whose purpose in marriage was primarily, or indeed wholly, the ordinary and true purpose of marriage, with residence in the United Kingdom as an incident of that marriage which was necessary and perhaps exactly what he wanted.' (p.7).

Lord Prosser went on to consider proposition 9 of *Hoque and Singh*, arguing that in such a situation, it would be even more fatally easy to treat an applicant's admission of his wishes to settle in the UK as evidence of the primary purpose of the marriage. However,

'It would be silly as well as cynical to believe that where a marriage brings advantages, the acquisition (or conferring) of those advantages must be seriously regarded as the primary purpose of the marriage, justifying not only the marriage itself, but lifelong union.' (p.12).

It is significant that Lord Prosser criticised the adjudicator for failing to 'attempt to weigh his part of the evidence against the whole of the rest of the evidence' (see Scannell 1992:5). He himself had clearly taken a more detached view of the applicant's evidence, which he saw as honest, strong and coherent, and he put in a strong word for granting the appellant's application (p.13) before remitting the matter to the adjudicator.

Unfortunately, as Scannell (1992:5) has emphasised, *Mohammed Safter* is 'but one decision flowing against the tide'. An openly hostile approach to the dilemma of South Asian women in Britain was adopted by the Court of Appeal in *Sumeina Masood* ([1992] ImmAR 69). In this case, decided on 9 July 1991, the wife had made it a condition of the marriage that the husband should come and join her. She was born and had lived all her life in Halifax, West Yorkshire. The parties got married in Pakistan on 15 January 1987 and the husband had been refused entry clearance on 27 July 1988. The wife had a job in Britain, her own house, and there was no question of her settling in Pakistan, though she had visited the country twice before. The parties were first cousins and it was an arranged marriage in accordance with custom, though the fact that the man wished to move to his wife's place was challenged as a violation of custom.

During the interview in Islamabad, the applicant's father had made a clear statement to the effect that the marriage had been arranged so that his son could go to live in the UK. The young man himself was less certain about this, but was obviously aware that his wife was not willing to settle with him in Pakistan. An impression was therefore building up in the mind of the entry clearance officer that this particular marriage would only be successful if the husband was allowed to come to the United Kingdom (see p.74). Referring to the unreported Tribunal decision in *Ashfaq Ahmed* (5258) on this point, where it was held that a marriage which was dependent upon a visa was clearly struck by the primary purpose rule, the ECO refused the application.

Lord Justice Glidewell, in *Sumeina Masood*, seemed to suggest first of all that the primary purpose rule indeed presumes, even if that may not be quite the appropriate word, 'but the sense is clear' (p.76), that fiancés and husbands will be desperate to come to Britain. Based on this assumption, it would appear, he challenged counsel's submission on the exercise of discretion (p.75), a further attempt to emphasise the legitimacy of the relevant rules which had come under challenge in *Rajput* by the same counsel. The Court of Appeal is here, it seems, almost overreacting in a defensive manner. Next it was found, on the basis of the evidence provided, that,

> 'it followed that the obtaining of an entry clearance certificate for the husband was a necessary precondition to him being able to live with his wife.' (p.77).

In other words, though this is not said, the genuineness of the marriage appears to be challenged. In essence, if the marriage depends on the granting of entry clearance for one of the spouses, as it indeed does if the British spouse is unwilling to live in the subcontinent, then there can only be a kind of conditional intention to live together, while the final decision to do so depends on the granting of the requisite entry clearance. From what was said in court, it is not clear what went through the minds of the judges. What we can see is that Glidewell LJ swiftly dealt his final blow to the case, relying on the concession, made by counsel,

> '...that an intention on the part of a party to the marriage to live permanently with the other conditional upon the other being able to obtain the necessary consent to enter the United Kingdom is no proper intention at all... It is the expression of a wish, but a wish only becomes an intention when there is some reasonable prospect of it being fulfilled.' (p.77-78).

Glidewell LJ thus agreed that the entry clearance officer had come to the right conclusion on the evidence before him when he took the view that the marriage was entered into primarily to obtain admission to the United Kingdom. He explained further:

> 'In this case, not to put too fine a point on it, the wife had the whip hand. She was the person who was saying quite firmly, 'I am established in the United Kingdom, I am a British citizen, I have a job, and I have a home. I very much hope that you can come and join me, but I am not going to live with you permanently unless you can'.' (p.78, also cited by Scannell 1992:5).

Having argued, as cited above, that an intention to live permanently with one's spouse which is conditional upon a spouse being able to obtain the necessary permission to enter the UK was no proper intention, the conclusion was reached that such arrangements were really entered into primarily to obtain admission and were thus hit by the primary purpose rule. On this, Glidewell LJ commented:

> 'The adverb 'primarily' in that passage is an important one. I know that it puts some intending immigrants in a very real difficulty, but it is not enough for somebody like Mr. Khalid Masood to convince the entry clearance officer that

he likes his wife, it may be he even loves her though that question did not arise in this case, and that if given the chance he intends to make a permanence of his marriage. This could be a perfectly genuine longlasting marriage. But that is not enough. If those considerations were secondary, the primary consideration was that he should first come into the United Kingdom. That was the primary purpose of the marriage, and if the entry clearance officer was not persuaded to the contrary, then he was entitled to refuse consent.' (p.78).

In other words, the Court of Appeal is here saying that a decision over who may and who may not immigrate to the United Kingdom as a spouse is ultimately a matter not for the individuals concerned, no matter what their legal rights may be, but for the state and its officials. Who, one almost reads, is Mr. Masood, a little Pakistani baker, to challenge the British immigration policy to keep down the numbers of male South Asians coming to Britain? This decision illustrates that courts tend to favour the government over the immigrants, even where immigrants' important interests such as liberty, livelihood and family unity and reputation are at stake (Legomsky 1987:49).

This openly illiberal decision, refusing to consider the position and the legal rights of the young woman as a British citizen by birth, was only possible because the parties were of South Asian origin. One is tempted to argue that no court in Britain would dare to come to the same conclusion if the spouses had been English.

Rick Scannell (1992:6) has commented that the effect of this decision cannot be overstated and that it creates a situation,

'in which a British citizen (or someone settled here) is unable to marry and be joined in this country by his or her spouse unless the former is content not to live in the United Kingdom.'

In the February 1992 issue of *Legal Action* (p.19), Rick Scannell suggests that *Sumeina Masood* may have been decided *per incuriam*, since it disregards the earlier, and better, authority of *Hoque and Singh*. Scannell explains this by arguing that 'Glidewell LJ is fundamentally mistaken in treating evidence of the wife's wish as to the place of matrimonial residence as evidence (adverse to the husband) of the primary purpose of the marriage.'

It is obvious that this decision not only affects the rights of young Pakistanis or South Asians, but of everyone. The Court of Appeal's present position, as Scannell (1992:6) emphasises, necessitates an appeal and it can only be hoped that a spirit of sympathy, which seems to have gone missing, will return. It is certainly no coincidence that after *Sumeina Masood* the need to look beyond domestic remedies became a matter of some urgency. If human rights were so clearly disregarded in the domestic forum, could one look to the EEC for a more human rights-oriented approach?

After Scannell wrote, a judgement by Schiemann J, sitting alone in the Queen's Bench Division, in *R. v. Immigration Appeal Tribunal ex parte Mohd Amin* ([1992] ImmAR 367) does give some cause for hope. Here an appeal was successful despite the negative decision of the Court of Appeal in *Sumeina Masood* ([1992] ImmAR 69). The adjudicator had rejected the husband's application because she did not believe what was put to her and described it as 'an incredible arrangement' (p.374). The problem here was that the British Muslim wife, already the mother of a young child from the husband, who was still in Pakistan, had proposed that her husband, who was from a traditional background, should stay at home and look after the child while she went out to work. Schiemann J made some interesting comments, first of all, about the existing law:

> 'Whether or not I am strictly bound to follow the approach in the decision in *Masood*, I do not think it would be right for me sitting at first instance to refuse to follow the unanimous approach of that court, far reaching as it is in its implications.' (p.373).

However, there was evidence that the adjudicator had not indicated in sufficient detail how her decision had been arrived at. For example, there was some evidence that the applicant had asked the wife to stay with him in Pakistan. This, if true, would be a powerful indication that the marriage was not entered into primarily to obtain admission to the UK (p.374). It might indicate that the wife had the 'whip hand', as Glidewell LJ had put it in *Sumeina Masood*, but she had apparently not explicitly made residence in the UK a precondition for the marriage. The facts were, thus, not fully identical with *Sumeina Masood*.

The learned judge proceeded to declare himself unhappy with the way in which the adjudicator had reached her decision. He suggested that,

> 'Adjudicators should indicate with some clarity in their decisions:
>
> (1)   what evidence they accept;
>
> (2)   what evidence they reject;
>
> (3)   whether there is any evidence as to which they cannot make up their mind whether or not they accept it;
>
> (4)   what, if any, evidence they regard as irrelevant.' (p.374).

In fact, Schiemann J goes further in suggesting that entry clearance officers should adopt the same approach (p.374). The final decision, namely to leave discretion to the Tribunal whether or not to grant leave to appeal poses an interesting question that remains unresolved at the time of writing.

■ 4.10 The dangers of pleading love

In view of insinuations that many if not most South Asian marriage arrangements are only made for entry clearance purposes, what if a couple is simply in love, or is pleading straightforward love? We do not know, of course, in how many cases this argument has been successfully used, but they cannot be many, firstly because most cases get rejected anyway and secondly, because to plead love is probably not quite in line with South Asian concepts; love is supposed to grow after marriage and not before. But where the primary purpose rule keeps spouses apart, how can matrimonial bliss develop?

The reported cases show immense reluctance on the part of the British judiciary to get involved in this issue, probably for fairly obvious reasons in terms of genuineness of a marriage, but also because some judges fail to understand South Asian concepts of the relationship between two spouses. The argument in cases, therefore, often avoids this question and gets side-tracked into other issues, notably economic factors.

In *R.* v. *Immigration Appeal Tribunal ex parte Manjula Jethva* ([1990] ImmAR 450), decided by Mr. Justice Popplewell in the Queen's Bench division on 10 May 1990, we find an alleged 'love marriage'. The wife, a British citizen, had gone to India for a visit and met the husband at a circus in May 1985. They fell in love and were married on 27 June 1985. It is apparent from the facts of the case (p.451) that the husband belonged to that class of people in India who are so poor that they could not afford a wife. He had never asked his wife to stay with him in India, and simply explained her unwillingness to stay in India by saying that it was too hot for her. The entry clearance officer made strenuous efforts to spot discrepancies in the couple's love story, found the husband's version lacking conviction and credibility, and became convinced that the husband had economic motives. The adjudicator also found himself convinced that if the man, a road worker, was too poor to marry in India, there was an obvious economic motive in marrying a woman from abroad.

On the question of love marriage, the adjudicator relied on an earlier unreported case, *Pindi Dass* v. *The Secretary of State for the Home Department* (5388). In it, the IAT had stated:

> 'In the experience acquired by the Tribunal in the course of many appeals such as this, of marriages between persons from the Indian sub-continent, a marriage contracted for reasons of personal emotions is a rarity, even taking into account the westernization of second-generation immigrant families. By this we mean nothing derogatory, and it may well be that arranged marriages have many advantages.' (p.454).

Based on this, Popplewell J came to the firm conclusion that, because in the Indian sub-continent arranged marriages are the norm, it was a 'necessary consequence' that 'love matches' are not the norm' (p.455). The Judge also made explicit comments about the level of judicial expertise in Britain on this matter:

159

'The Immigration Appeal Tribunal is probably the most experienced tribunal in relation to marriages that exists in the world. Even those of us who sit doing Crown Office work have some familiarity with arranged marriages.' (p.455).

Counsel for the husband sought to develop the argument that a 'love match' in the sub-continent was clearly not the same as understood in Western European society, but the judge was unwilling to listen. The interview notes disclosed that the couple in this case had spent some time together talking about love, though the wife objected to the intrusive questioning and refused to disclose what precisely had been said.

The judge's comments are worth reproducing here, since they show the typical inability to appreciate non-Western patterns of thought and action:

'Falling in love is a perfectly normal concept which is understood by everybody in the world, and I do not imagine that falling in love is any different in India than it is in this country; these two people contend that they had in fact fallen in love.' (p.455).

Nobody in this case talks about consummation of the marriage, or premarital cohabitation, or indeed some hidden romance behind a dam, as one might be tempted to imagine. The learned judge was unwilling to probe any further, but certainly not because of respect for the privacy of the spouses: here is unwillingness to go into the substance of the matter, despite the claimed judicial expertise, because it might help the husband to establish that it was not his primary purpose to seek immigration to Britain. The case comes to a remarkably swift conclusion when Popplewell J refuses to criticise the adjudicator for not understanding what a 'love marriage' or a 'love match' is and says:

'It seems to me the answers which they gave suggested that they had fallen in love in the normal way that those words are understood.' (p.456).

It is not made clear by what twist of logic such a conclusion justifies the dismissal of the appeal. In another recent case, *R. v. Secretary of State for the Home Department ex parte Jagdishchandra Jinabhai Prajapati* ([1990] ImmAR 513), the wife had gone through an earlier arranged marriage, which had proved disastrous. She then met a young man whom she liked and decided to choose her own spouse this time, hoping for the best. The man worked in Muscat, and the wife's failure to follow him there raised suspicions of primary purpose.

The adjudicator refused to believe the wife's account of what he called 'the supposedly whirlwind romance' (p.516). In view of two years of separation till the couple were eventually reunited for a while, the image of a love match seemed strange. Despite clear evidence of intervening devotion in the form of letters and phone calls, and even though the sponsor was pregnant by the time the matter came before the IAT, the conclusion remained that the husband's primary purpose was suspect.

In *R. v. Immigration Appeal Tribunal ex parte Shivprasad Bhagwandas Gondalia* ([1991] ImmAR 519), the couple had been badly advised in a situation which is quite typical:

'Apparently, or so it is said, on advice received by an agent in India, they started off in an effort to persuade the entry clearance officer that this marriage was a love-match between them.' (p.520).

The wife went to India on 20 October 1987 and met the applicant for the first time seven days later. After another week, the marriage had been fixed, and on 29 November 1987 the couple were married. The wife then returned to England some six weeks later. The speed of these arrangements raised the usual suspicions about 'convenience', with no reference to holiday schedules and other reasons why the wife might have had to return to the UK.

The spouses then communicated by letter and the wife 'tutored' the husband about how to respond in the interview in Bombay. The husband subsequently 'told the concocted story that this was a love-match' (p.520). The 'story' was repeated by the wife at her interview in England, but the entry clearance officer, at the husband's second interview, found that this marriage was in fact arranged, since the woman was said to be a total stranger and the man, in view of his economic situation, had a clear 'economic incentive to leave India' (p.521). After the appeal to the adjudicator had been filed, the spouses admitted that their account had been fabricated and that the marriage had, in fact, been an arranged marriage.

The adjudicator, in a carefully worded decision, found clear evidence of strong intervening devotion:

'This intervening devotion casts a favourable light on this case. It is not detrimental to the appellant's case that the sponsor may have posed an advance condition that she would only marry a man willing to come and live with her in the United Kingdom.' (p.522).

However, the 'reduced credibility' (p.523) of the applicant and the sponsor inevitably became a major consideration. The adjudicator now saw 'an enormous economic incentive' (p.523), and Henry J in the Queen's Bench Division went further in emphasising the poor economic background of the applicant:

'We know from the papers that even if he had earned three times as much he would still not be at the level requiring him to pay income tax. Therefore, it cannot possibly vitiate the essential factual finding that he came from a poor economic background and had 'an enormous economic incentive' to make a marriage.' (p.523).

The result of this case was predictable. It illustrates the dangers of bad advice, but also shows that 'love' will not overcome immigration barriers, while the barriers will get even higher when there is evidence of an 'economic incentive' for the man.

The way in which the arguments in the above case developed shows that little regard will be paid to human sentiment, while economic considerations have acquired a greater role. This is evidenced by a growing number of cases in which rejection is justified on the basis of the maintenance and accommodation requirements, as indicated before and emphasised by Jim Gillespie (1992). One such typical case is *Entry Clearance Officer, Islamabad* v. *Mohammad Jahangir Hussain* ([1991] ImmAR 476), in which the ECO won the appeal on the basis of challenging the rather tentative maintenance and accommodation arrangements for the applicant.

Our research has shown that there are few other reported cases that contain a discussion of 'love marriages' among South Asians. The issue does not figure prominently in Macdonald and Blake (1991) either. Phil Powell (1992: Sheet 4) in fact cites the above statements from *Manjula Jethva* and then proceeds to provide quite detailed material that throws light on the South Asian perceptions of a 'love marriage'. Powell emphasises the influence of romantic formulae and stereotypes nurtured by the film industry, so that 'love' is largely imagined and anticipated, and may be based on 'no more than the brushing of hands, a somewhat clandestine meeting, or a silent exchange of looks'. But is this less real than love based on close contact? Powell's concluding comment puts a question mark over the findings in *Manjula Jethva*:

> 'But even when they greatly exaggerate the romance — 'we walked alone, hand in hand, at the local beauty spot' — the young men never mean a love relationship in the western sense.'

This also raises the question whether our courts are justified in rejecting all evidence of 'love' among South Asians, just as they appear to be marginalising evidence of intervening devotion and, at least in one case, of prenuptial devotion. In *R.* v. *Immigration Appeal Tribunal ex parte Jasmine Miah* ([1991] ImmAR 184) a young Bangladeshi man claimed that his marriage was a love match and that the couple, who had had time to meet before the marriage, had actually built up a genuine relationship prior to marriage, which should have been a relevant factor to be taken into account. However, since the case contained other intricacies, the argument was not pursued with enough vigour; the negative outcome of the case was predictable in view of the immigration history of the husband.

A recently reported case involves a woman from the Philippines who had married an Englishman. This, as Cotran et al. (1991:IV 45H-46) tell us in their most recent update, is one of the first decisions involving Anglo-Philippine marriages to be heard on appeal by the High Court. Apparently, there have been a large number of such liaisons. Many couples have found the wife's application rejected, and there will, it appears, be many more such decisions in the near future.

Here we see reflections of a much less hostile approach to the applicant than in many of the cases referred to above involving Indians and Pakistanis. Yet the result, till the adjudicator stage, was the same: rejection of the applicant's appeal on the ground of primary purpose, here in essence based on a suspicion that the woman's devotion might not be genuine, but rather 'meretricious' (p.413), which is surely a big word for 'fake' or, as Schiemann J put it, part of 'an elaborate attempt by Victoria to deceive Mark' (p.413). Clearly, *R.* v. *Immigration Appeal Tribunal ex parte Victoria Ofiana Hansford* ([1992] ImmAR 407 'is somewhat out of the usual run', as the adjudicator had phrased it (cited at p. 409) and the tone is much more gentlemanly. It appears that the wife's application to join her husband in the UK had been rejected to give a signal that there are no open floodgates for Filipinas. The adjudicator, at any rate, had commented that such appeals 'may become more common as there appears to be a fairly active contact between the West Midlands and the Philippines' (p.409).

Schiemann J., in the Queen's Bench Division, found himself tempted, as everyone else, to presume that this was a primary purpose case (p.412). But, says the learned judge:

> 'It is all too easy for those of us regularly engaged in poring over the entrails of these marriages to assume that the primary purpose of marrying an Englishman is to obtain admission to the United Kingdom. To jump to that conclusion, as I confess I did in the course of argument, in the absence of any other evidence and without the point ever having been put to Victoria is not fair to her and not fair to Mark.' (p.412).

Not only is the tone refreshingly different here, and fairness is explicitly emphasised, it is also quite apparent that the aggressive questioning technique of entry clearance officers in Islamabad or anywhere else in the subcontinent has not been followed in this case. The wife had simply never been directly challenged to tell anyone, it appears, whether her primary motive was to come to the UK. Most likely her primary purpose was to marry a nice Englishman, which is of course very different from saying that someone wants to marry a nice Pakistani or Indian girl (or man, for that matter) from Britain!

Some judicial dissatisfaction with the whole process of deciding such appeals shines through what Schiemann J says about the process of interpreting the evidence. He comments on the fact that the adjudicator, 'as is usual in this rather strange process,' (p.411) never saw Victoria. When considering the question of devotion, the adjudicator similarly seems to complain about lack of first-hand evidence:

> 'In the whole of this somewhat inspissated matter I see nothing from her to suggest that the marriage had not been entered into primarily to obtain her admission to the United Kingdom. In fact what followed from joining the quasi matrimonial bureau mostly points in the opposite direction.' (p.413).

The adjudicator was probably indicating here, through posh words hiding some embarrassment, that this was a sticky matter. In legal parlance, the argument had to be put differently to come to a positive finding. Schiemann J concluded:

> 'It is manifestly not an inevitable conclusion from a girl's desire to marry an Englishman that any subsequent marriage to an Englishman was entered into primarily to obtain admission to the United Kingdom.' (p.415).

It was also helpful to the applicant that the adjudicator had not pressed the issue of economic incentives, though there is some indication that this point was indeed considered:

> 'I am satisfied that the applicant is not being impelled here by poverty but it is inescapable in the majority of appeals of this sort that there will be financial and material benefit from coming here.' (p. 412).

It is highly improbable that an adjudicator would have left the matter at that if it had been a South Asian applicant seeking to join an Asian spouse in the UK. It remains to be seen how this kind of case will be decided in the future.

Of course, the fact that in the above case the intending immigrant is the female spouse and that the man is an Englishman, may be presumed to make a significant difference. That case also did not afford an opportunity to consider the vexed question of modification of custom, since there is nothing unusual about women from the Philippines joining a man anywhere in the world.

In cases from the subcontinent, however, the closely related matter of custom and obedience to tradition has, quite naturally, become much more central than the issue of love. This is only natural, since it centres on the question of choice of matrimonial home. It figures prominently in many cases, is discussed in detail by Powell (1992 and before) and receives some attention in Macdonald and Blake (1991:264). The whole issue is, of course, very closely linked to the dilemma of a *Sumeina Masood* situation, where the wife makes it a condition of the marriage that the husband joins her, rather than the other way round.

There can be no doubt that South Asian traditions favour the patrilocal pattern, but this does not mean that matrilocal or indeed neolocal arrangements, where the couple start off in a new place of their own, are outside the norm. As Macdonald and Blake (1991:264) rightly emphasise and illustrate with good examples, there are neither religious prescriptions nor rigidly binding customary norms that force South Asian women to join the men in their place of residence. There is no violation of custom here, but a shift in customary traditions, to the extent that even Muslim women, as we saw above, might argue openly that they are prepared to be the breadwinner. In this context, it is worth re-examining our stereotyped perceptions of South Asian women as dependents of men. Anyone who has been to the subcontinent and has seen the large numbers of working women must have begun to doubt whether the convenient middle-class image of the obedient housewife is in fact a reflection of a myth rather than social reality.

The Home Office stance that husbands joining wives in Britain exploit a devious departure from South Asian customs, designed to circumvent the strictness of British immigration controls, is obviously questionable in a variety of ways and needs to be challenged more vigorously. But it is equally obvious that it remains fatally easy to take a male applicant's answer that he is ready to come to the UK to join his wife as an admission of primary purpose of the marriage. The conundrum that this rule poses remains unresolved in favour of the Home Office, mainly because of the rules on the burden of proof. The most recent update to Cotran et al.(1991) also contains very detailed statistics from the Home Office about the numbers of persons admitted to the UK in 1991. The details provided here show that significant numbers of spouses from the subcontinent continue to apply for entry clearance. Obviously such statistics must be grist to the mill of those who seek to exercise the tightest possible immigration control. 27% of acceptances in 1991 were from the Indian subcontinent. Figures of 19,000 wives accepted for settlement, as well as 11,600 husbands are given for 1991 (Cotran et al. 1991: D 49). Though the numbers are not high in absolute terms, they are portrayed as rising, creating an impression of threat. No doubt, such figures will be used to justify further attempts at fine-tuning the existing system of immigration control for spouses. At present, though, the easiest way is simply flexible use of the burden of proof, to allow a semblance of legality, while no applicant can be sure of success, however convincing his or her case may appear.

■ 4.11 Relief from Europe?

Recourse to European law is not a new feature of British immigration law. We noted that in 1985, the issue of sex discrimination in the Immigration Rules between those pertaining to husbands/fiancés and wives/fiancées resulted in action before the European Court of Human Rights in the case of *Abdulaziz, Balkandali and Cabales* v. *U.K.* ([1985] 7 EHRR 471). As we saw, at that time the UK government had advanced the argument that its Immigration Rules as pertaining to husbands/fiancés were needed to protect the domestic labour market, but this did not succeed. A significant part of the ruling was that the UK had failed to offer effective domestic remedies to those who complained of injustices resulting from administrative practice. While the requirement under the Rules that the parties to a marriage must have met was held not to be racially discriminatory, the Court also rejected a breach of article 8 of the European Convention on Human Rights, which concerns the right to family life, since the Convention does not guarantee an absolute right to enter a member state (see Macdonald 1987: 300-302; now Macdonald and Blake 1991:244 and 331-334).

Recourse to European law, as well as to international human rights instruments, will therefore always come up against the claim of primacy of national discretion. Much of the current debate about Maastricht has, of course, precisely to do with the fear of impairing national sovereignty over such important matters as border controls and determining immigration policies. Freedom of movement within the EEC, also for third country nationals once they are in the territory of the EEC, has now become a matter of focal interest and great concern.

Since direct recourse to human rights protection mechanisms was not likely to be a meaningful remedy for tackling the effects of the primary purpose rule once gender discrimination had been rectified in 1985, a different strategy was developed during the late 1980s and early 1990s. Nuala Mole outlined the possibility of using a European route, little noticed at first, to circumvent the effects of the primary purpose rule in Britain:

> 'Where the UK resident is a British citizen, he/she is also an EEC national and consequently free to take a spouse to any EEC country. This alternative to residence in Africa or Asia may be more attractive and more realistic and the couple may be willing to contemplate making their home in, for example, the Republic of Ireland if they are to be refused the right to live together in the UK.' (Mole 1987:34).

The issue was raised in *R.* v. *Immigration Appeal Tribunal ex parte Ahmad Aradi* ([1987] ImmAR 359). The applicant was a citizen of Iran and had married a woman who held dual nationality. She was both a British citizen and a citizen of the Republic of Ireland. The man had been in Britain before 1982, returned as a visitor in 1984, and married her on 4 October 1984. He had been given only temporary admission to the UK and was now seeking to rely on his marriage to an EEC citizen to assert freedom of movement rights.

In essence, the husband claimed the right to enter the UK 'so as to join and live with his wife, who is working here' (p. 360). The difficulty was, though, that the wife had never even been to Ireland. Would her husband be able to use provisions of EEC law on free movement?

Webster J in the Queen's Bench Division considered various provisions of EEC law and found that there was nothing in EEC law that applied to the situation of Mr. and Mrs. Aradi. The fact that Mrs. Aradi had never exercised or sought to exercise any right to freedom of movement under Article 48 of the Treaty of Rome meant that she, or her husband, could not rely on the freedom of movement provisions. To fall under those provisions, one had to exercise the right to movement first. The wife could not simply argue that, as a dual national living in one country, she had more or less automatic coverage from the other, since this would create a class of privileged EEC citizens, as the IAT had noted (p.362).

After this case, it was quite clear what a couple separated by the primary purpose rule in Britain would have to do. The British spouse would have to move to another EEC country, exercising her right to freedom of movement. She could then be joined by her overseas spouse, in accordance with the laws of that EEC country, which in most cases allowed more or less instant family reunion. The question to be answered was for how long the couple would have to live in Germany, France, or any other EEC country before they could enter the UK as a couple.

Testing this took several years. In the meantime, a growing number of British Asian wives have moved to the continent to be united with their husbands. Many such women work there, and many appear to have decided not to return to the UK at all. If, however, the couple wanted to live in the UK, what would the position be? The recent case of *Surinder Singh*, now reported as *R. v. Immigration Appeal Tribunal and Surinder Singh ex parte Home Secretary* ([1992] 3 All ER 798) and also found in Cotran et al. (1991: VI 109-121), has given a definitive answer to this question.

In this case, which was not exactly a primary purpose case, the relevant principle is nevertheless established. The facts are that an Indian Sikh man had married a British Sikh woman in 1982, they had both worked in Germany between 1983 and 1985, and they had returned to the UK at the end of 1985 to open a business. The husband was granted limited leave to remain as the husband of a British national in 1986. But the couple's marriage broke up and in July 1987 a decree nisi was pronounced. Thereafter, the husband found it impossible to obtain indefinite leave to remain in the UK and was in fact subject to a deportation order made in December 1988. The decree of divorce was made absolute in February 1989. However, the IAT had allowed the husband's appeal from an adjudicator in view of the husband's claim to a right under EEC law. The question arose, therefore, whether Community law granted a right of residence to a national of a non-member country, or third country national, who was the spouse of an EEC national returning to work in his or her own country after having worked in another member state.

The outcome of this case was awaited with great interest and it was positive. On 7 July 1992, the European Court of Justice in Luxembourg held that,

'Article 52 of the EEC Treaty and Council Directive (EEC) 73/148 required a member state to grant leave to enter and reside in its territory to the spouse, of whatever nationality, of a national of that state who had gone, with the spouse, to another member state in order to work there as an employed person as envisaged by art 48 of the Treaty and returned to establish himself or herself as envisaged by art 52 of the Treaty in the state of which he or she was a national.'

It was also held that the third country national spouse was entitled to at least the same rights as would be granted to him or her under EEC law if his or her spouse entered and resided in another member state. (Cotran et al. 1991: VI 110).

While this case secured the desired right to Mr. Singh in the present case, the decision was hailed variously as a challenge to UK immigration law and as undermining the primary purpose rule. In effect, of course, the primary purpose rule is still in full force and no real damage has been done to British immigration control. It is clear, however, that the decision of the ECJ means that the many British Asian couples exiled to a European country can now settle in Britain if they wish. It is also clear that couples facing separation due to the primary purpose rule are well-advised to consider taking up residence in another EEC country.

In its most recent Annual Report, the JCWI (1992:6) has commented:

'This now leaves the law in a still more illogical position: British citizens have no right under British immigration law to bring their foreign spouses to the UK, but those who have lived and worked for some months, with their spouses, in another EC country do have this right. *Surinder Singh* makes the case for the abolition of the primary purpose rule even stronger.'

In fact, the *Surinder Singh* case has led to a change of policy by the Home Office which does not take away the primary purpose rule, but seeks to mitigate some of the worst effects of that rule. It can be seen as 'too little too late', but is a meaningful concession for many long-suffering couples. It was announced in Parliament on 30 June 1992 that fresh guidance had been issued to Home Office staff in the light of judicial rulings on the relevance of evidence of 'intervening devotion' in primary purpose cases, thus avoiding, one suspects, an impression that the changes were introduced as a result of the outcome in *Surinder Singh*. The effect of this is that:

> '...an application from a spouse for an entry clearance or for leave to remain should be allowed when it is accepted that the marriage is genuine and subsisting and either the couple have been married for at least five years or one or more children of the marriage have the right of abode in the United Kingdom. An application might nevertheless be refused, for example, where the applicant's criminal record would make his or her exclusion conducive to the public good or where the sponsor in the United Kingdom is unable to meet the maintenance and accommodation requirements of the Immigration Rules. It is not possible to estimate accurately the number of applicants who may be affected by this guidance.' (Cotran et al. 1991: D 49).

It will be noted that this change of policy involves consideration of the rights of British citizen children in such cases, who are deprived of the right to family life. The policy change, thus, is probably also a pre-emptive strategy to avoid a further case under EEC law. In addition, explicit reference to the maintenance and accommodation requirements underlines what we found earlier, namely a definite strengthening of the economic considerations in the context of immigration.

The *Leicester Rights Bulletin*, No. 64 (September/October 1992) confirmed that several clients' husbands had, as a result of these changes, been issued entry clearances. Welcome as this may be, the problem itself has not disappeared. The JCWI Annual Report 1991/92 (1992:8) comments on this with a mixture of relief and scepticism:

> 'JCWI welcomes this change for the effect it will have for couples who meet its criteria and who may now be reunited after many years of misery and separation, but we are sceptical about the long-term effects and about how it will be operated. As the rule is used primarily against applicants from the Indian subcontinent... we fear that there will now be an unofficial five-year waiting period for couples in these areas, operating as a disguised quota system to regulate migration.'

The apprehensions voiced here are not at all far-fetched. A quota system has for some time been in operation when it comes to making applications in the first instance, be it for visitors or for applications by spouses. The recent Home

Office statistics (see Cotran et al. 1991: D49 -D77) clearly indicate lengthening queues, which are of course, at least partly, the result of stricter quota regulations and are, as it were, a new form of creative accounting which has come under criticism from the JCWI and others.

Clearly, the primary purpose rule is so central to British immigration control that it is unlikely to disappear completely. The point of detail that is not settled at the moment is for how long a British national would have to remain in an EEC country to trigger off the freedom of movement provisions. There may be more scope in exploring EEC law than we imagine at the moment.

On the domestic front, in the current climate of increasing phobia about any form of immigration, the minds of entry clearance officers, which are after all the major control mechanism for applications by spouses, will not be opened — rather the opposite. The legal remedies, as this study shows, have been restricted so severely, and have been fine-tuned so effectively, that even on appeal there is now only limited hope of sympathetic consideration.

Appendix:

Chronological list of Immigration Rules 1973-1990

Control on entry — Commonwealth, 1973, H.C. 79
Control after entry — Commonwealth, 1973, H.C. 80
Control on entry — aliens, 1973, H.C. 81
Control after entry — aliens, 1973, H.C. 82
Immigration Rules, 1977, H.C. 238-241
Proposals for change, 1979, Cmnd. 7750
Immigration Rules, 1980, H.C. 394
Proposals for change, 1982, Cmnd. 8683
Immigration Rules, 1982, H.C. 66
Statement of Changes in Immigration Rules, 1983, HC 169
Statement of Changes in Immigration Rules, 1985, H.C. 293
Statement of Changes in Immigration Rules, 1985, H.C. 503
Statement of Changes in Immigration Rules, 1986, H.C. 306
Statement of Changes in Immigration Rules, 1986, H.C. 584
Statement of Changes in Immigration Rules, 1987, H.C. 154
Statement of Changes in Immigration Rules, 1987, H.C. 208
Statement of Changes in Immigration Rules, 1988, H.C. 555
Statement of Changes in Immigration Rules, 1989, H.C. 388
Statement of Changes in Immigration Rules, 1990, H.C. 251

Index of Cases

Abdulaziz, Cabales and Balkandali v. U.K [1985] 7 EHRR 47   81, 84, 91, 165
Afzal (4784)   135
Alexander v. I.A.T. [1982] 2 All ER 766   30
Anseereeganoo [1981] Imm AR 30   88
Ashfaq Ahmed (5258)   155
Attorney-General for Canada v. Cain [1906] AC 542   14
Begum [1978] ImmAR 174   110
Bhatia (see Vinod Bhatia and R. v. IAT ex parte Vinod Bhatia)
Channo Bi [1978] Imm AR 182   110
Cheema see R. v. IAT ex parte Cheema
Class-Peter [1981] ImmAR 154   88, 110
Devesh Dhirubhai Patel v. E.C.O., Bombay (4373)   128-129
East African Asians v. United Kingdom [1981] 3 EHRR 76   81
Entry Clearance Officer, Islamabad v. Mohammad Jahangir Hussain   162
   [1991] ImmAR 476
Farouq (4505)   128
Gama Singh (4902)   135
Hayat (4651)   128
Hirani v. Hirani [1983] 4 F.L.R. 232 CA   74
Hisham Ahmed Ali Abdel Rahman v. Secretary of State for the Home
   Department [1986] ImmAR 405   135-6
Home Office v. Commission For Racial Equality [1985] QB 385   36
Hoque and Singh see IAT v. Amirul Hoque...
Hosenball see: R. v. Secretary of State
IAT v. Amirul Hoque and Matwinder Singh [1988]   134-5, 139-144,
   ImmAR 216   147, 150, 155, 157
Ilyas Yacub Patel v. Secretary of State for the Home Department   136
   [1986] ImmAR 440
Khanom [1979-80] Imm AR 182   110
Kulwinder Singh (4946)   135
Lambhikar Singh (3353)   120, 121
Mahmud Khan [1983] QB 790 and [1982] ImmAR 134 CA.   59, 62, 88

Manjit Singh v. ECO New Delhi [1986] ImmAR 219 — 136
Matwinder Singh (unreported, DC 16 March 1990) — 153-4
Matwinder Singh (6136) — 153
Mohamed v. Knott [1969] 1 QB 1 — 111
Mohamed Numanul Islam Choudhury v. IAT [1990] ImmAR 211 — 151
Mohammad Afzal v. Visa Officer, Islamabad [1986] Imm AR 474 — 135
Mohammad Malik [1981] Imm AR 134 — 62
Mohammad Shahban v. Visa Officer, Islamabad (6996) — 2
Mohammed Safter v. Secretary of State for the Home Department
[1992] ImmAR 1 — 154-5
Musgrove v. Chun Teeony Toy [1891] AC 272 — 14
Naresh Kumar (3278) — 119, 121
Narinder Singh Sandu (4352) — 128, 129
Nathvani [1979-80] Imm AR 9 QBD — 57
Naushad Kandiya v. IAT and Aurangzeb Khan v. IAT
[1990] ImmAR 377 — 150-1
Osama [1978] Imm AR 8 — 62
Papayianni [1974] Imm AR 7 — 48, 80
Pearson [1978] Imm AR 212 — 29
Pervez Iqbal v. IAT [1988] ImmAR 469 — 144
Pindi Dass v. The Secretary of State for the Home Department (5388) — 159-160
Prajapati v. I.A.T. [1982] Imm AR 56 (CA) — 30
Prasadhkumar 1992 [1] Kerala Law Times 729 — 110
R. v. Chief Immigration Officer, ex parte Salamat Bibi — 29
[1976] 1 WLR 979 (CA)
R. v. I.A.T. and Surinder Singh ex parte Home Secretary — 3, 80, 105, 110, 166-8
[1992] All ER 798
R. v. I.A.T. ex parte Ahmed Aradi [1987] ImmAR 359 — 166
R. v. I.A.T. ex parte Arun Kumar. [1986] — 130-4, 135, 137-142, 146-7
ImmAR 446 (CA)
R. v. I.A.T. ex parte Bashir (DC) 15 March 1988 — 143, 150
R. v. I.A.T. ex parte Cheema [1982] ImmAR 124 (CA) — 59
R. v. I.A.T. ex parte Davesh Pranjivan Desai [1987] ImmAR 18 — 136-7
R. v. I.A.T. ex parte Hardev Singh Dhillon [1987] ImmAR 385 — 137
R. v. I.A.T. ex parte Jasmine Miah [1991] ImmAR 184 — 162
R. v. I.A.T. ex parte Khatab [1989] ImmAR 313 — 146, 150
R. v. I.A.T. ex parte Kulbandar Kaur [1990] ImmAR 107 — 154
R. v. I.A.T. ex parte Lunat (6 October 1986, QBD) — 145-6
R. v. I.A.T. ex parte Manjula Jethva [1990] ImmAR 450 — 159, 162
R. v. I.A.T. ex parte Matwinder Singh (The Times, 15 April 1987) — 139
R. v. I.A.T. ex parte Mohammad Bashir [1984] ImmAR 165 — 129

R. v. *I.A.T. ex parte Mohd Amin* [1992] ImmAR 367 — 158

R. v. *I.A.T. ex parte Najma Rafique* [1990] ImmAR 235 — 152-3

R. v. *I.A.T. ex parte Naushad Kandiya* [1989] ImmAR 491 — 151

R. v. *I.A.T. ex parte Shameem Wali* [1986] ImmAR 86 — 146, 150

R. v. *I.A.T. ex parte Shivprasad Bhagwandas Gondalia* [1991] ImmAR 51 — 161

R. v. *I.A.T. ex parte Sudash Bala Garg (The Times* 17 March 1989) — 144

R. v. *I.A.T. ex parte Sukhjivan Singh* [1988] ImmAR 527 — 145

R. v. *I.A.T. ex parte Ullah* [1982] ImmAR 124 (CA) — 62

R. v. *I.A.T. ex parte Victoria Ofiana Hansford* [1992] ImmAR 407 — 162-4

R. v. *IAT ex parte Vijay Kumar* (23 February 1989) — 143-4

R. v. *IAT ex parte Vinod Bhatia* [1985] Imm AR 39 QBD — 123-4, 125

R. v. *Secretary of State, ex parte Hosenball* [1977]
1 WLR 766 (CA) and [1977] 3 All ER 452 — 29

R. v. *Secretary of State, ex parte Jagdishchandra Jinabhai* — 160
Prajapati [1990] ImmAR 513

Rajput see Yogeshkumar Shantilal Rajput v. *IAT*

Rashida Bibi v. *IAT* [1988] ImmAR 298 — 153

Ravinder Singh (3352) — 120, 121

Salamat Bibi see R. v. *Chief Immigration Officer*

Schmidt v. *Home Secretary* [1969] 2 Ch 149 — 10

Shaukat Ali (unreported, DC 13 February 1992) — 154

Sopariwala v. *E.C.O.*, Bombay (4318) — 128-9

Sukhinder Singh (5329) — 152

Sumeina Masood v. *IAT* [1992] ImmAR 69 — 110, 116, 120, 155-8, 164

Surinder (3128) — 120

Surinder Singh see R. v. *I.A.T.* and *Surinder Singh*

Syed Jabar Hussain Shah (6033) — 152

Tanveer (3456) — 88

Thakrar [1974] QB 684 — 27

Ullah see R. v *IAT ex parte Ullah*

Vasilejevic [1976] ImmAR 44 — 57

Vervaeke v. *Smith* [1983] AC 145 [1982] AllER 144 — 55

Vinod Bhatia (3456) — 88, 123, 125

Vinod Bhatia v. *I.A.T.* [1985] ImmAR 50 (CA) — 123-4, 125-6,
128, 130, 131, 140, 147

Yogeshkumar Shantilal Rajput v. *IAT* [1989] — 3, 30, 147-150, 156
ImmAR 350 (CA)

Zahra [1979-80] Imm AR 48 — 111

Table of Statutes

Aliens Act, 1905	8, 16, 20
Aliens Act, 1919	16
Aliens Order, 1920	17
Aliens Restriction Act, 1914	8, 16
British Nationality Act, 1948	9, 18, 28
British Nationality Act, 1981	35, 66, 81
Commonwealth Immigrants Act, 1962	7, 9, 10, 20-22, 27, 32, 45, 112, 120
Commonwealth Immigrants Act, 1968	9, 10, 23-25, 27, 32, 46, 49, 66
Hindu Marriage Act, 1955 [India]	110
Housing (Homeless Persons) Act, 1977	94
Immigration Act, 1971	9, 10, 25, 26, 27-31, 32, 35, 40, 44, 50-51, 57, 70, 98, 100, 102, 104, 123, 147-8
Immigration Act, 1988	9, 29, 40-42, 101, 111
Immigration Appeals Act, 1969	25, 47
Immigration and Nationality Act, 1952 [USA]	19
Polish Resettlement Act, 1947	17
Race Relations Act, 1965	22, 34
Race Relations Act, 1968	22, 35
Race Relations Act, 1976	22
Special Marriage Act, 1954 [India]	138

Bibliography

Aurora, G. S. [1967]: *The new frontiersmen*. Bombay: Popular Prakashan.

Ballard, Christine [1978]: 'Arranged marriages in the British context'. In: Vol.6 No.3 *New Community*, pp. 181-196.

Banton, Michael [1988]: *Racial consciousness*. London and New York: Longman.

Berger, Vincent [1989]: *Case law of the European Court of Human Rights*. Vol I: 1960-1987. Dublin: The Round Hall Press.

Bevan, Vaughan [1986]: *The development of British immigration law*. London et al: Croom Helm.

Bhabha, Jacqueline, Francesca Klug and Sue Shutter [eds.] [1985]: *Worlds apart. Women under immigration and nationality law*. London and Sydney: Pluto Press.

Blake, Nicholas and Richard Scannell [1988]: 'The Immigration Bill: just the limited reinforcement of the 1971 Act?'. In: *Immigration and Nationality Law and Practice*, Vol. 3 No.1 [April 1988], pp. 2-4.

Bradford, Keith [1975]: 'Marriage by proxy'. In: Vol. IV, No.2 [Summer 1975] *New Community*, pp. 254-255.

Bradley, David [1983]: 'Duress and arranged marriages'. In: Vol. 46 *Modern Law Review*, pp.499-504.

Bromley, P.M. [1981]: *Family law*. Sixth edition. London: Butterworths.

Bromley, P.M. and N.V. Lowe [1987]: *Family law*. Seventh edition, London: Butterworths.

Carroll, Alex J. [1991]: 'The Gulf Crisis and the ghost of Liversidge v Anderson'. In: *Immigration and Nationality Law and Practice*, Vol. 5 No.3 [July 1991], pp. 72-76.

Commission for Racial Equality [1985]: *Immigration Control Procedures. Report of a formal investigation*. London: CRE.

Cotran, Eugene, David Pearl and Alper Riza [1991]: *Butterworths Immigration Law Service*. Looseleaf Folder. London: Butterworths.

Desai, Sunderlal T. [ed.] [1982]: *Mulla's Principles of Hindu law*. Fifteenth edition, Bombay: N.M. Tripathi.

Drabu, Khurshid and Stephen Bowen [1989]: *Mandatory visas. Visiting the UK from Bangladesh, India, Pakistan, Ghana and Nigeria*. London: Commission for Racial Equality.

Dummett, Ann [1973]: *A portrait of English racism*. Harmondsworth: Penguin.

Dummett, Ann and Andrew Nicol [1990]: *Subjects, citizens, aliens and others.* London: Weidenfeld and Nicholson.

Evans, J.M. [1983]: *Immigration law.* Second edition. London: Sweet and Maxwell.

Foot, P. [1965]: *Immigration and race in British politics.* Harmondsworth: Penguin.

Fransman, Laurie [1989]: *Fransman's British nationality law.* 2nd ed. London: Fourmat.

Fryer, P. [1984]: *Staying power: The history of black people in Britain.* London: Pluto Press.

Gainer, B. [1972]: *The alien invasion.* London: Heinemann.

Gillespie, Jim [1986]: 'The new Immigration Rules'. In: Vol.1 No.1 [April 1986] *Immigration and Nationality Law and Practice,* pp. 23-25.

Gillespie, Jim [1990a]: 'The consolidated immigration rules: a review of the changes in HC 388'. In: Vol.4 No.1 [January 1990] *Immigration and Nationality Law and Practice,* pp.14-16.

Gillespie, Jim [1990b]: 'Still more new immigration rules: a review of the changes in HC 251'. In: Vol. 4 No.2 [April 1990] *Immigration and Nationality Law and Practice,* pp. 75-78.

Gillespie, Jim [1992]: 'Maintenance and accommodation and the immigration rules: recent developments'. In: *Immigration and Nationality Law and Practice,* Vol. 6 No. 3 [July 1992], pp. 97-100.

Gorlick, Brian [1991a]: 'The exclusion of 'security risks' as a form of immigration control: law and process in Canada'. In: *Immigration and Nationality Law and Practice,* Vol.5 No.3 [July 1991], pp. 76-82.

Gorlick, Brian [1991b]: 'The exclusion of 'security risks' as a form of immigration control: law and process in Canada — Part II'. In: *Immigration and Nationality Law and Practice,* Vol.5 No.4 [October 1991], pp. 109-115.

Grant, Lawrence [1987]: 'Applications by husbands, wives and fiancé(e)s'. In: Vol. 2 No.2 [July 1987] *Immigration and Nationality Law and Practice,* pp. 26-32.

Grant, Stephanie [1987]: 'Family rights in UK and EEC immigration law'. In: Vol. 2 No.2 [July 1987] *Immigration and Nationality Law and Practice,* pp. 38-40.

Griffith, J.A.G. [1991]: *The politics of the judiciary.* Fourth edition. London: Fontana.

Hood Phillips, O. [1978]: *Constitutional and administrative law.* 6th ed., London: Sweet and Maxwell.

Jackson, J.A. [1963]: *The Irish in Britain.* London: Routledge & Kegan Paul.

Joint Council for the Welfare of Immigrants [1977]: *Checks on immigrant marriages.* London: JCWI.

Joint Council for the Welfare of Immigrants [1992]: *Annual Report 1991-92.* London: JCWI.

Jones, Mervyn [1956]: *British nationality law.* Oxford: Clarendon.

Kannan, C.T. [1978]: *Cultural adaptation of Asian immigrants: First and second generation.* Greenford: Author.

Krausz, Ernest [1972]: *Ethnic minorities in Britain.* London: Paladin.

Lal, Sushma and Amrit Wilson [1986]: *But my cows aren't going to England.* Manchester: Manchester Law Centre.

Layton-Henry, Zig [ed.] [1990]: *The political rights of migrant workers in Western Europe.* London et al: Sage.

Leech, K. [1966]: *'Migration and the British population, 1955-62'.* In: Vol. VII, No.4 *Race* pp.401-408.

Legomsky, Stephen [1987]: *Immigration and the judiciary. Law and politics in Britain and America.* Oxford: Clarendon.

Lester, Anthony and Geoffrey Bindman [1972]: *Race and law.* Harmondsworth: Penguin.

Macdonald, Ian A. [1972]: *The new immigration law.* London: Butterworths.

Macdonald, Ian A. [1987]: *Immigration law and practice.* 2nd ed. London: Butterworths.

Macdonald, Ian A. and N. Blake [1982]: *The new nationality law.* London: Butterworths.

Macdonald, Ian A. and N. Blake [1991]: *Macdonald's immigration law and practice.* 3rd ed. London: Butterworths.

Macmillan, H. [1973]: *The end of the day.* London: Macmillan.

Marrett, Valerie [1989]: *Immigrants settling in the city.* London: Leicester University Press.

Marrington, Dave [1985]: 'Legal decisions affecting ethnic minorities and discrimination — No.24'. In: Vol. XII, No.3 [Winter 1985] *New Community*, pp. 536-545.

Marrington, David [1988]: 'Legal decisions affecting ethnic minorities and discrimination — No.29'. In: Vol. XIV, No.3 [Spring 1988] *New Community*, pp. 460-468.

Menski, Werner F. [1987]: 'Legal pluralism in the Hindu marriage'. In: Burghart, Richard [ed.]: *Hinduism in Great Britain.* London: Tavistock, pp. 180-200.

Menski, Werner F. [1988]: 'English family law and ethnic laws in Britain'. In: 1988(1) *Kerala Law Times*, Journal section, pp. 56-66.

Menski, Werner F. [1990]: 'South Asian laws in British legal practice: a matter for immigration lawyers?' In: Vol.4 No.2 [April 1990] *Immigration and Nationality Law and Practice*, pp. 63-67.

Menski, Werner F. [ed.] [1993]: *Coping with 1997. The reaction of the Hong Kong people to the transfer of power.* Stoke-on-Trent and London: Trentham Books.

Menski, Werner and Rajesh Bhavsar [1992]: 'Author and subject index to INLP Vol. 6 [1992]'. In: Vol. 6 No.4 [October 1992] *Immigration and Nationality Law and Practice*, pp. 144-148.

Mole, Nuala [1987]: *Immigration: Family entry and settlement.* Bristol: Jordan & Sons.

Montgomery, Caroline [1989]: *Asian women and homelessness in Britain.* London: SOAS [LLB Essay].

Moss, Peter R.H. [1988a]: 'Statement of changes in Immigration Rules HC 208 — a short note'. In: Vol. 3 No.1 [April 1988] *Immigration and Nationality Law and Practice*, pp. 17-18.

Moss, Peter R.H. [1988b]: 'Statement of changes in the Immigration Rules HC 555: a note for practitioners'. In: Vol. 3 No.3 [October 1988] *Immigration and Nationality Law and Practice*, pp. 54-56.

Newdick, Christopher [1985]: 'Immigration, marriage and the primary purpose rule'. In: *New Law Journal*, 16th August 1985, pp. 816-818.

Peach, C. [1965]:'West Indian migration to Britain: The economic factors'. In: Vol. VII No. 1, *Race*, pp.31- 36.

Peach, Ceri [1968]: *West Indian migration to Britain*. London: Oxford University Press.

Pearl, David [1986]: *Family law and the immigrant communities*. Bristol: Jordan & Sons.

Pearl, David [1987]: 'South Asian immigrant communities and English family law'. In: Vol. XIV, No.1/2 [Autumn 1987] *New Community*, pp. 161-169.

Poulter, Sebastian [1986]: *English law and ethnic minority customs*. London: Butterworths.

Poulter, Sebastian [1987]: 'Ethnic minority customs, English law and human rights'. In: Vol. 36 *International and Comparative Law Quarterly*, pp. 589-615.

Powell, Phil [1990]: 'Custom and tradition in primary purpose cases: does the ECO really know best?'. In Vol. 4 No.3 [July 1990] *Immigration & Nationality Law & Practice*, pp.107-109.

Powell, Phil [1991]: *Notes for UK immigration lawyers on custom & practice in the Indian sub-continent*. Issue No.5 [November 1991], London.

Powell, Phil [1992]: *Notes for UK immigration lawyers on custom & practice in the Indian sub-continent*. Issue No.6 [November 1992], London.

Rees, Edward [1989]:'Recent judicial developments on 'primary purpose''. In: Vol. 3 No. 4 [January 1989] *Immigration and Nationality Law and Practice*, pp.92-94.

Ross, Matthew and Werner F. Menski [1992]: 'Subject index to I&NL&P Vols 1-5 (1986-1991)'. In: Vol. 6 No.1 [January 1992] *Immigration and Nationality Law and Practice*, pp.i-xvi.

Rose, E.J.B. et al. [1969]: *Colour and citizenship. A report on British race relations*. London et al: OUP for IRR.

Roth, C. [1964]: *History of the Jews in England*. Third edition. Oxford: Clarendon Press.

Scannell, Rick [1990]: 'High Court decisions. Primary purpose'. In: Vol. 4 No. 4 [October 1990], *Immigration and Nationality Law and Practice*, pp. 147-148.

Scannell, Rick [1992]: 'Primary purpose: the end of judicial sympathy'. In: Vol. 6 No.1 [January 1992], *Immigration and Nationality Law and Practice*, pp. 3-6.

Shah, Samir [1979]: 'Asian marriages: A case of white propaganda'. In: *New Society* 18 October 1979, pp.132-133.

Sharma, V. and F. Wooldridge [1974]: 'Some legal questions arising from the expulsion of the Ugandan Asians'. In: Vol. 23 *I.C.L.Q*, pp.397-425.

Shutter, Sue [1992]: *Immigration & nationality law handbook*. London: JCWI.

Simon, Julian L. [1989]: *The economic consequences of immigration.* Oxford: Basil Blackwell.

Sondhi, Ranjit [1987]: *Divided families. British immigration control in the Indian subcontinent.* London: Runnymede Trust.

Steel, David [1969]: *No entry. The background and implications of the Commonwealth Immigrants Act 1968.* London: Hurst & Co.

Supperstone, Michael [1983]: *Immigration: The law and practice.* London: Oyez Longman.

Survey of Leicester 1983: Initial report of survey. Leicester: Leicester City Council.

Thornberry, C. [1962]: 'Law, opinion and the immigrant'. In: Vol. 25, pp. 654-671. *M.L.R.*

Tilbe, D. [1972]: *The Ugandan Asian crisis.* London: British Council of Churches.

Uganda Resettlement Board [1974]: *Final Report* [Cmnd. 5594]. London: H.M.S.O.

Uganda Resettlement Board [1973]: *Interim Report.* London: H.M.S.O.

UKIAS [1987]: *Annual Report 1986-87.* London: UKIAS.

UKIAS [1988]: *Annual report 1987-88.* London: UKIAS.

Vincenzi, Christopher and David Marrington [1992]: *Immigration law. The Rules explained.* London: Sweet & Maxwell.

Visram, Rozina [1986]: *Ayahs, lascars and princes.* London et al: Pluto.

Wade, E.C.S. and A. W. Bradley [1985]: *Constitutional and administrative law.* Tenth edition. London and New York.

Walvin, James [1971]: *The black presence.* London: Orbach and Chambers.

Waters, Robert [1990]: *Ethnic minorities and the criminal justice system.* Aldershot et al.: Avebury.